Finding the Answers to the Problems of Life

INTUITIONS

Seeing With The Heart

Finding the Answers to the Problems of Life

INTUITIONS

Seeing With The Heart

Winter

For Down Publishing

430 Simpson Road
Saco, Maine 04072

Published by Tor Down Publishing
430 Simpson Road, Saco, Maine 04072

Second Edition

Cover Photography by Susan Mills, Bowdoinham, Maine

Library of Congress
Cataloging-in-Publications Data

ISBN 0-9636992-0-2

To My Father . . .
Who Taught Me to be Quiet

Acknowledgements

As with any book, there are many individuals I would like to thank for their support and help in revising, editing and publishing this second edition of *Intuitions:*

Michael, my best friend, advisor, confidante, lover, and partner, for his continuing support and faith in my abilities; Jackie and Ed Robinson, my in-laws, for helping me break my paradigms about what parents (and in-laws) should and shouldn't be; Kent Flowers, for his incredible generosity; Caroline Tilton for her work with the layout; and Jean Templeton for her generous time and energy to make this book readable.

I give a special note of thanks to Denise Herzing, *Stenella* and crew of the Wild Dolphin Project; Joy Hampp, Laura Urian, Deb Huckabee, and the staff at the Dolphin Research Center; and all of my finned friends who continue to show me what life and freedom are about and who are so willing to teach me. I am sure that long after this edition is out I will be remembering you.

Especially you, **Natua** and **Annessa.**

Contents

Day three:
Stenella

Wild Dolphin project:

There is nothing like the first encounter with a dolphin in the wild. It is an unexpected delight to be with something this special. Before breakfast I walked onto the deck and spotted a "fin" moving through the waves a few yards from the stern of the boat. "Dolphins," I called and soon everyone was jumping into their masks and fins and plunging over the side of Stenella, a 62' catamaran, into the midst of a pod of spotted dolphins. Within seconds I found myself just "hanging" next to a male (later identified as Skew) watching, observing and being observed. The fact that they will come so close . . . amazing. How comfortable I have become with jumping off the side of a boat into the water because the call of dolphins goes out. How quickly I ignore the fact we saw a large tiger shark in these same waters just yesterday. How quickly I notice that my mind wants to label the dolphins good and the shark bad when, in fact, they are both parts of nature . . . the yin and the yang of it. The shark has as much right to be here as the dolphins; he (or she) also has a story to tell.

Intuitions was first created and published in 1988, telling of my initial encounters with expanded awareness, dating back to childhood and into the early '80's. With this present edition many more things have taken place; my life has moved in many new (and yet similar) directions. I seem to be moving from the "me" to the "us" phase of awareness and, I think that this is a very good thing for me. It would be difficult to understand and know about the universe without going inside, and yet at the same time we must be aware that there is more, whether we project it out or whether it is already there in another reality isn't the question. As life continues to unfold I constantly remind myself that what has become "normal" to me actually, to many individuals, isn't normal, but falls into the category of make believe. Here, in the early 1990's many things are taking place very rapidly on the planet, a new awareness of GAIA, of looking for something more . . . a connection to the earth. The cold war is over and people are talking about their search for meaning.

Things are changing–the question is are we ready for the change and can we meet the challenge? Can we change our way of thinking, suspend our disbeliefs and create new paradigms in order to meet the challenge?

Dolphins

The Second Edition of *Intuitions* wouldn't be complete without a section on the environment, and for me, some of my biggest mentors . . . the dolphins. I once heard Kelli McGee, one of the educators at the Dolphin Research Center say, "The dolphins call us, and when they do you can't hang up."

In 1990 Michael, my partner and husband, became interested in dolphins. He has always been an advocate of wildlife and very interested in nature, the ocean and its mysteries. When he met a friend who was involved in some exciting research with dolphins, it grabbed his attention, and through a series of synchronistic events he found himself in a program at the Dolphin Research Center in the Florida keys. As a result of his contact with them we began to combine our workshop on Intuition with a week-long dolphin swim.

"What is it like to be with the dolphins?" you might ask.

I would reply, "I really can't tell you; you'll just have to experience them for yourselves."

When I first met the dolphins I had given very

little thought as to why so many individuals wanted to swim with them. I probably felt that they were similar to most animals with whom we have a great telepathic rapport. However, to recount all of the ways that dolphins have shown me there is more to our universe than meets the eye would take a book in itself, and couldn't do justice to them or to my experience. I can say that there has been more than one occasion when the dolphin I was with very clearly read my mind.

My first experience of this kind was with a dolphin named Annessa, a dolphin that, I soon learned, loved to tease and "stretch" humans in many different ways. Annessa and her lagoon partner Aleta had just given me a long dorsal pull, practically taking me to Cuba from Grassy Key. After deciding that it was time to obey their trainer's whistle, they tipped their rostrum down, their massive gray bodies descended below the surface, and my hand slipped from their dorsal fins. I found myself thinking:

"I'm so far out here, why don't they take me back?" The moment, or millisecond, that I formed this question in my mind, Annessa was there, her dorsal fin pushing against the palm of my hand. No words could have made the message clearer: "Take hold and I'll take you back!" I knew then, from the depth of my being, that there was much more to dolphins than I had imagined . . . ever.

Two other experiences that week showed me just how elementary we humans are at communication. The first experience came with a dolphin named Natua. Natua was a movie star, the most practiced at being in movies, and the center of much of the re-search into dolphins' understanding human language. I was giving Natua and two other dolphins a signal in response to a question I had asked. Delphi and Kiby responded to my signal in an appropriate manner, but Natua just looked at me, not moving.

"What's wrong, Natua?"

I waited for a response, when all at once I had a total knowing that was as if a picture within a picture within a picture came into my awareness. The question that I had asked did not fit with the signal I was giving. I changed the signal and Natua responded with a behavior appropriate to my original question. Signals and behavior, just *who is* doing the learning? Certainly not Natua.

In that moment I knew that not only could dolphins read my mind, but also I could understand messages that they sent. And I realized that they can send incredibly complete messages by mental telepathy. Natua had sent me a mental picture that encompassed layers of information. It was an instant "Knowing," showing me how little we know about the workings of our own mind and how little we know about the mind of the dolphin. I later read about Swedenborg, a seventeenth century Swedish mathematician, who would communicate with the "angels" when he meditated. He described their communication as a telepathic burst of knowledge, a picture language so dense that each image contained a thousand ideas. This was the way Natua had communicated with me in that moment.

The third and final experience of my first week with dolphins came with Misty. Misty is an older dolphin and one that can frequently be contrary. All week Misty had preferred the absence of humans and had demonstrated this by hanging out in the far corner of her pool. On this particular morning she called to me using her signature whistle as I was walking down the lane. I was so surprised I didn't believe that it was Misty, but Deb (one of the DRC staff) yelled to me, "Misty is calling you."

I tentatively moved over to Misty's dock and sat down. I waited. Nothing. I waited longer. Nothing.

Finally, after twenty minutes or more, I decided to try to communicate with her by placing a single, clear thought (this simplicity was for me, not her) in the center of my mind and sending it out. I felt awkward as I tried to formulate a question that would be appropriate, respectful, and not too much trouble for her. At the same time I was anxious to know if she could or would *read* my mind and respond.

"Misty, I really hate to ask you to do this, but I am trying to understand how to communicate with you, and, ummm, would you mind, horribly . . . I mean I know you probably don't feel like it, but would you mind? If you can understand me, would you please swim by the dock to show me that this stuff works?"

She did.

More recently I had been spending all of my free time with Marina as she attempted to teach? me her sounds. (I won't say language because I am not sure that is what it is.)

Everything had led up to this week, far beyond the sight of land in the Bahamas. I sat, waiting, watching the contour of the emerald green water. I realized that I do know when dolphins are near, even if I can't consciously hear or see them. I know, and that is an affirmation for me.

"Now," you might ask, "Why is there a chapter on dolphins in a book on intuition? Why talk about dolphins in the forward to the book?"

Because dolphins show us our connectedness, something we need to get back in touch with if we are to survive, just like our intuition. It's all the same. We are them and they are us. Carl Sagan wrote in 1973,

"If we can't understand dolphins in their environment, with their intelligence, how can we expect to understand a being who comes from another planet, someone we wish to call alien?"

I am now, more than ever, convinced that the word intuition has a depth to it, just as the dolphins have a depth to them, that we will probably never understand, no matter how much we study and observe them, or how much we study and observe our intuition.

Approach your intuition just as you would approach a dolphin, gently. Come into its environment with an openness to discover what's there. Listen, learn its language, not the language you would put onto it.

I think that intuition is a desire to connect, just as the dolphins want to connect. Use your curiosity, your desire to know, to understand, to discover your inner world. And, if the dolphins call you, know that you won't be able to hang up!

*Toto, I've a feeling
we're not in Kansas anymore.*

Dorothy, *The Wizard of Oz*

Winter

One: If You Believe in Fairy Tales . . .

Once upon a time when dreams came true and imaginary playmates were something to be "reckoned" with, there lived a little girl who lived in a house in the woods with her parents. Quite often the little girl would wander the woods with her friends (that only she could see) playing Indian or, better yet, "Little Red Riding Hood." In those days magic was an everyday occurrence, for the little girl could summon up rainstorms at will, and doctor and make well almost any of God's creatures that found the good fortune to be at her healing hands.

On days when she was very, very lucky, her father would take her fishing. It was there that he taught her to be quiet. Otherwise she would not be able to hear the fish when they wished to talk with her.

On the days when she was not so lucky her father would head off to the golf course to have a "round" of golf. "My dear," he would say, "Golf is like the game of life. Every round is a journey which ultimately leads you back to exactly where you began. The ball is a symbol of perfection in that it contains all potential because it is a sphere. When it is in flight it is a reminder to us that we can fly, if we but put our minds to it. If you can learn to focus your mind, and send that little white ball exactly where you want it to go, then you can focus your life and create it exactly as you would have it be. Do not begrudge me my game of golf, for there in that simple game is the possibility of finding the true secret of life."

I was that little girl.

There would be times when my parents and I would pack our bags and head off to Georgia to visit my grandparents. This trip was likely to take place any time during the year, always on a moment's notice, when my father decided he could leave his business for a few days. It never failed that when we would arrive dinner would be waiting, hot, on the table. This in itself always amazed me because we had been driving for hours and I knew that we hadn't called to tell my grandmother when we would arrive. In fact, she didn't have a telephone. When I would ask how did she know to have dinner on the table, my parents would reply, "She just knows." Yet, she didn't even *know,* rationally, on what day we would arrive.

It would not be unusual during our visit for my grandmother to refer to the noise upstairs as being made by someone who had long since "left this plane" or to speak of seeing the "fairies dancing in the rain." All of this was very normal to me, and my parents were wise enough not to say whether they did, or didn't, believe in what grandmother said.

I quickly discovered, once I started school, that other children didn't believe in Santa Claus, let alone believe in ghosts and fairies. I was definitely in the minority.

Those first years of school were difficult for me. Whenever the teacher would write a math problem on the board, I always knew the answer, but I didn't have a clue as to how to "work" the problem; so I was always accused of cheating. I would also be accused of eavesdropping because I would know information that I shouldn't know. "If you hadn't been listening you wouldn't know this." I soon learned it was best to keep my mouth shut and not say what I knew or thought.

As I look back through my childhood, I can re-member just "knowing things" but not relating this knowledge to psychic ability. I remember the time I knew that a lost child was sitting on the side of a lilypool and if I didn't get to him, he would fall in and drown. I thought I was able to stand in my yard and look down at the pond and see him, but in reality there was no way I could stand in my yard, look through the forest and down a hill and see him. I remember "knowing" that another childhood friend was going to die, and when he did, thinking that I had caused it. I would frequently see pets that had died as they walked around my home or slept on their favorite chair. My mother tried to tell me that I saw them because I expected to see them. One day I saw my grandmother sitting in a chair at our home, not a place I expected to see her. When I told my mother this she stopped telling me I saw things because they met my expectations. Somewhere during all this, I began to add a line to my prayers; after blessing all of my animals, and all of the animals, and all of the people, I added "and please don't let me see a ghost."

I also remember that my biggest fear throughout those years was that my father was going to die and leave me. When, at age sixteen, he died, I shut down all of my emotions. After all, what good does it do to love someone? They just leave you.

The death of my father came as a surprise to me, my mother, and all of those who knew him. He was young and seemingly in good health, although he did smoke too much. I remember awaking at 12:23 a.m. and knowing that my father was dead. (I was away at the time.) I got up, packed my bag and waited for the phone call which would bring me the news. The entire time this was going on I felt his presence with me, as real in that form as it had ever been in life. When the phone call did come, the information was that he was very ill and had been taken to the hospital. Of course I knew better, because his spirit was beside me giving me the information I needed for the coming days.

When I arrived home, my mother, who had become hysterical, had been sedated, and I was informed that I would have to make the funeral arrangements. Me. I had never been to a funeral in my life. I didn't know the first thing about where to bury my father. North Carolina or Georgia, what type of casket, or worse yet, how much money did we have to do those things? My father stood at my shoulder and calmly told me what to do—where to buy a plot, what casket to pick, and what music and other arrangements for the funeral he wanted. People who came to our home thought I was either cold or in shock because I showed no grief. How can you show grief when the person who has died is there helping you through a tough situation?

The night of the funeral my father asked me to come sit at the head of the stairs where we had had our last long conversation. "You and your mother are going to be fine and it is time for me to go on. There is an insurance policy I want you to call about that will take care of you and your mother." Then I felt him pull away.

The next day I called about the policy, and the company informed me that he had come in the previous week and taken out a policy, but he had not come back to sign it. I insisted that they pull the policy and check. When they did, it was signed.

I had a similar experience with someone else who had passed on that same year. I had a magnificent piano teacher who, for the first time in my life, had awakened the musical talent in me. I adored this teacher and thought that my whole world depended on his teaching me forever. I had never played so well nor enjoyed it as much as at that time in my life. One evening, after a particularly successful recital, I said to him, "Mr. Young, what would I ever do without you? I have learned so much and there is so much more I need to know." I'll never forget his reply, "I've taught you all I know. All you need to do is practice."

The next day he committed suicide.

Two weeks later I was scheduled to play in a state

music competition. I was refusing to go because I had not practiced and I felt there was so much more I needed to know before I was ready. But my mother and friends encouraged me to go ahead, saying that Mr. Young would have wanted it that way. The night of the competition I sat down at the piano, ready to make a complete fool of myself and not caring. The audience was packed. There must have been over a thousand people there ready to see some incompetent teenager try to prove she could play the piano.

Just before I began, I looked to my right, and there, standing beside the piano was Mr. Young. He smiled and said, "It's all right. You'll do fine."

I played that evening in a way that I had never played in my entire life. It was one of those magical states where the piano played me. When it was over I was told again and again that people listening thought it was Mr. Young at the keys. I didn't tell them that I thought it was, too. Mr. Young won the competition that night.

These events were a normal part of my growing up. I didn't think that they were unusual, or that I had any unusual talents or skills. I had always believed in fairy tales and magic. Those who didn't just didn't see "clearly."

Two: The "Real World"

I don't remember when I forgot the magic. Somewhere between Psychology 213 and Logic 101, I fell into the "real" world. My life became caught up with parties, the Viet Nam War, graduate school, and a host of other things. My magical world fell by the wayside as "reality" and the need to make a living became my focus.

Interestingly enough, I never had trouble making money or getting "just the right job at just the right time." In fact, my motto was, "I'm always in the right place at the right time." I didn't realize that this was an affirmation and that I was, indeed, creating my reality . . . and doing a pretty good job of it as long as I didn't give my power away to a nay-sayer. You know the type: "You'll never get that job, you're too young, inexperienced, female, etc." When I listened to them, and believed what they had to say, I didn't get the job. When I listened to myself, I did.

Throughout my life I seemed to always create interesting, flexible jobs. The one thing I learned early on was that I am a free spirit and I need a sense of freedom and autonomy in order to function at my best. As I went from working in the public school system to therapist/ researcher/educator to university instructor and stopping as analyst with the office of the Attorney General, I knew I wasn't doing what I was supposed to be doing. It was always as if I were preparing for something else. Thinking that in order to prepare you take courses, I was always enrolled in one degree program or another, never finishing, usually becoming bored as soon as I got into it. To this day I am amazed I hold any degrees, especially at the Master's level, because my attention span was always so short. There was also another part of me that said, "This isn't the real knowledge. This is superficial."

It was while working in the legal field that the magic came back into my life. I began to realize that I wasn't happy. Usually it had been my experience that when I wasn't happy I would automatically make a change. After making the change, my mood would shift and I would realize I had not been happy doing whatever it was that I was doing. This time I actively realized I wasn't happy. I would sit at my desk and ask, "Why am I not happy? I have a wonderful, excit-ing position with the Office of the Attorney General— a position that many lawyers would be envious of. I have access to a past and present governor on a first-name basis, as well as to most of the agency heads within the state. I am working on a First Amendment case that is challenging and never dull. I make a good salary; I am married to a handsome, intelligent, kind individual; I had nice clothes, a nice home, car . . . all of the material things a person could ask for. What's missing?"

Life, of course was missing. My spirit was crying to be set free and I didn't know it. I would sit in my office and feel an unseen chaos all around me. I couldn't see it, but I knew that it was there.

One day Linda, one of my co-workers, came into my office with a book. "I thought you'd like to look at this," she said.

It was a copy of the *I Ching*. Although I had never heard of this book, I quickly became fascinated with it. There, behind the closed doors of my litigation office, I fell into tossing coins in order to ask about my future. The first *I Ching* ever tossed landed on Hexagram Number One with no moving lines. The content of that message remains with me to this day. Essentially it said:

> Creating Power is nothing less than the detonating device in the evolutionary bomb. The time is exceptional in terms of inspiration, energy, and will. The force of this time is the primal directive that propels us into our destinies regardless of what our reasoning or recalcitrant minds may think. What you create now will be the basis and inspiration for what you experience next. As a result of any action you now take, your fate will be sealed. *You may always trace back to the beginning, but there will never be an end to what you are about to set in motion. (I Ching Workbook,* R. L. Wing)

I read the hexagram and felt a chill run through my body. Suddenly it was as if my world shifted and things were different. The experimental psychologist in me began to toss the coins again, not for more information but to figure the probability that the three coins would fall in this position six times. The message felt so right I couldn't believe it was an accident that I received this message at that point in time.

A few days later Linda mentioned that she and four other friends were going to see a "psychic." I had never been to a psychic and doubt that if I had thought about it I would have gone, because I probably would have feared that I would be told something tragic. As luck would have it, one of the four dropped out of their appointment and, on a lark, I decided to go. The last thing I said to my secretary as I left the office was, "She'll probably tell me I'm a psychic."

The first thing the psychic said to me when I walked into her presence was, "Why are you here? You're a psychic. You know the answers."

My experience with the psychic was truly amazing. I couldn't figure out how she knew what she knew . . . was she reading my mind? When I quizzed her on how I should find my psychic ability she replied, "I can't tell you that; that's the journey. You must find it for yourself."

So I began to read. In the three weeks before my First Amendment case was to come to trial, I read twenty-five books. No easy feat when you are working from sunup to midnight preparing for a major legal battle. But read I did, and I still didn't know how I was psychic. I would say things to people, thinking I was conveying psychic information, and it would turn out to be pure left-brain fiction. I was becoming increasingly frustrated with trying to figure out how this "thing" worked.

I did learn a couple of interesting things during this time in my life, however. Either there are no accidents or everything is an accident. And I discovered I had a voice in my head that spoke to me, a male voice that seemed somewhat muffled and far away, but a voice that would provide me with accurate information.

Three: Imagination is Real

One morning, just as I was awakening from sleep, frustrated and questioning what to do next, this voice told me to "look around Charlottesville." True to form, I stopped by the bookstore on my way to work. This was typical of my conditioning . . . the answers are in books and there must be another book that I need to read. When I entered the bookstore, I asked the owner a question, and before she could answer, the only other person in the store turned and answered the question. I immediately knew that this person had information that I wanted; *she* was why I was in the bookstore that morning, not for a new or better book.

It turned out that this person was a trainer at a place called the Monroe Institute. The institute is an educational and research organization devoted to the premise that "focused consciousness contains all solutions to the questions of human existence. Only through interdisciplinary approaches and research efforts can the understanding of this consciousness be realized."

I immediately went to my office and called the Monroe Institute for information about their program.

"I'd like to come out and see your facility and what you do."
"There's nothing to see," the pleasant voice at the other end of the telephone replied, "and we don't allow people to come through while a program is in progress."
"Can you tell me what you do there?"
"It's hard to explain on the telephone," the voice continued. "It's a process of using sound to balance the hemispheres of the brain." This

type of conversation, moving nowhere, continued for about half an hour. Finally I said, "Send me the application forms."

As I made this request, I wondered how I would find the time and the money to attend a week-long training program doing something I wasn't at all clear about. Following my newfound knowledge that there are no accidents, I figured that if I wasn't supposed to go, it wouldn't work out. I wouldn't have the money, the trial would go on longer than expected, or I just wouldn't be accepted into the program.

The trial, scheduled to last three weeks (this was the second attempt after many delays and one mistrial), ended three days early. I received a tax refund for the exact amount of the training, and naturally, I was accepted into the program.

If anyone had told me that I would spend the next week in a state of primary isolation listening to tapes over headphones, I would have said they were crazy. I was just this side of hyperactive, a manic personality, running seven to thirteen miles a day and never sitting still for more than fifteen minutes at any one stretch. I had no idea what I was letting myself in for.

I did go and I did listen to tapes for several hours a day. I began to see that my "imagination" was real; the pictures in my head gave me accurate information that could be used for messages both about myself and others. Of course, it was not until I was halfway through the program that I figured this out, and not without some help from a co-participant who put his arrowhead necklace in my hand and said, "Tell me what you see."

I immediately rattled off a series of pictures, in detail and color, that were going through my mind. He said, "That's me and that's my wife, house, etc." I couldn't believe it. I couldn't believe that the pictures and words that came into my mind gave me information I could trust—valid, reliable information.

This same individual encouraged me to take part in the research program there at the Institute, which I did. The training I received there as an "explorer" was invaluable to my growth as a psychic. There is nothing that can compare with being in a sensory-deprivation booth, listening to soothing sounds coming into my ears through headphones, and having two very well trained experts at the other end ask me questions about myself, the universe, and life in general.

It was also through my training at the Institute that I began to learn that we do receive the thought when someone else thinks of us, and we can "throw" energy wherever we desire. That healing and many other forms of communication are possible using this same form of energy.

Four: You Are More Than Your Physical Body

The entire time I was at the Monroe Institute training program I was trying to decide if I thought there was such a thing as an "out of body" experience or if it was simply remote viewing. While I did have some interesting experiences in the form of feeling my hands and arms lift out of my body, I couldn't say I knew what an OBE (Out-of-Body Experience) was. This was one of the many times I found myself asking the question and the powers that be giving me an answer, an answer in such detail I couldn't deny its validity.

I went with some friends to the home of a psychic that was going to channel. Not being in touch with modern-day channeling, I thought I could call in my father and ask him why I was afraid to be psychic . . . was there something I feared?

The evening was set with eleven other people, candles, and a doberman for good measure. The psychic asked that we all relax, a state very easy for me to accomplish, while she drew in her sources, but for some reason, she was unable to channel that evening. I know now that I was taking her energy. I had relaxed, and when I did, I pulled in large amounts of universal energy, including the energy around her.

After she was unable to get into trance, she began to go around the room and tell the participants what guilt they came into this life with. I will say now that that was not a positive thing to do; it promoted a judgment on behalf of the psychic which can draw lesser energies into the experience.

When she came to me, she began to talk about my fingers. (I am very sensitive about my fingers; I thought it was because I play the piano and was constantly told as a child to protect my hands). She said, "You were tortured. Your fingers were broken back and then chopped off!"

When I heard that, I immediately became myself dying as a witch. I was tied to a stake and as I felt the fire creep up around me I began to smother. I screamed, "It's not fair! It's not fair!" I saw that I had red hair and green eyes, I saw the individuals around me (one man who later told me he thought he lit the fire), and I noticed the sandy area. I felt that I was in New England.

The psychic jumped up and ran over to where I was. She waved her hands over me and I remember thinking, "This isn't helping." By then I was starting to leave my body. I wondered if it were possible for a soul to die in the same way twice.

While all of this was taking place, a woman in the room began to have an epileptic seizure. My thoughts left the "burning" to the thought that "I can heal her." I went to her, held her head in my hands, and her seizure stopped. At this point I began to feel a lot of negative energy in the room, and I found myself arguing about this with the psychic, who tried to persuade me that the energy wasn't negative. I knew I had to get out of there; so I left and went out and sat on her porch, putting my feet and hands on the ground and resting my head on my knees. It was raining and the rain felt good to my traumatized body.

Within a little while I became worried about a young girl who was back in the room with the psychic. I knew that she was afraid and that I should go to her and help her with her fears. I stood up, went to the front door, noticed the handle of the door, and then I moved into the foyer. I was aware that, although the doberman was standing beside me, he seemed to be ignoring me. This was unusual for this animal, who was usually nervous. Someone opened the door to the room where the meeting was and I moved quickly across the room to Sharon, the girl I came to help. I wondered why they had turned up the lights and why the doberman took such a circuitous route to come to the same place in the room where I was.

I took Sharon's hands in mine and told her she was safe, just to ignore the psychic and what was going on. I heard the psychic say, "Your fears have called the spirits," and she got up and began to move over to where we were. Not being particularly enamored of this psychic, I moved away.

The next thing I knew I was back on the porch and two of my friends were shaking me, asking me if I was all right. I found that I couldn't stand up. They carried me to their car and then up to my apartment and put me to bed. I awoke in the middle of the night and realized that I was still burning. My thought was, "Oh, no! You haven't counted yourself back to consciousness after relaxing at the beginning of the seance!" I counted back to one and the burning sensation went away.

The next day my friends told the following story. Once I left the room I did not return. After about an hour had passed the psychic said, "There's a spirit at the door. Let the spirit in." Someone opened the door and my friends saw a grey mass float across the room. The interesting thing was that when we questioned Sharon, whose eyes had been tightly shut because of her fear, she said, "Yes, Winter, you came to me and comforted me. You held my hands and I felt much calmer with you than I did with the psychic. I wish you hadn't left!"

I realized that not only had I been out-of-body, but my guardians had set me up in such a fashion that I couldn't deny what had taken place. How many individuals have eleven other people who can verify that they have moved around without any physical form?

The next evening I realized that it is probably harder to stay in your body than it is to get out of it. I decided to practice backing out by a method I had been taught at the Monroe Institute. I found it quite easy to back out, and as I stood by my bed, preparing to go somewhere, I was suddenly seized on the arms by four strong pinching hands. "Um," I thought. "Guess I'll stay home tonight." There have been other times I have suddenly found myself across a room staring back at my physical form and watching myself talking. On one such occasion, a male friend of mine had become, perhaps, a little too friendly. Not wanting to rebuff him, and wanting to maintain our friendship, I chose to move from the sofa where we were sitting and walk across the room. It was after I turned back to speak to him that I realized my physical body was still on the sofa. The interesting thing was that he knew I had left my body on that occasion and later called my attention to the fact.

Now, like most individuals who have discovered their OBE's, I work to consciously know when I am out. I had two instances of being out with friends happen during the same week. During the first instance one of my friends floated through the door of my bedroom and complained that her husband had said something to her that she didn't like. The second instance occurred a few days later, when I was visiting a good friend that I had not seen for several months. I was looking forward to having a glass of wine with him and catching up on his life as a resident. As luck would have it, when I arrived for the visit he had the worst cold he had ever had in his life. We had a quick dinner and he promptly went to bed, leaving me frustrated about all of the unspoken conversation I had planned.

Somewhere during the night I was aware of him floating through the wall and lying down beside where I was sleeping. I don't remember what was said, but the next morning I awoke with a wonderful sense of peace and the knowledge that we had been able to converse after all.

At first, I was upset that both of my friends had apparently been able to leave their bodies so easily while I was still in mine. Later I realized that I had to have been out of my body in order to see them.

Five: Masters

One sunny afternoon I was in my kitchen, calmly washing dishes,when I became aware that something else was present. So I turned to face the refrigerator. It was as if I were viewing Star Trek and hearing,"Beam me up, Scotty." I first saw glitter all around the base of the refrigerator, and then, slowly, I saw an eight foot tall being, with long grey robes, begin to take shape. No, I didn't say, "Oh, what a wonderful being you are," but instead I waved my hand and said, "Not now." The being quickly went away. This episode, more than ever, made me question the out-of-body state. Was this really a guardian, or a friend of mine, coming to visit without form?

I soon discovered that just because one sends away a being in a long grey robe doesn't mean that they don't exist. I think my guardians, or masters, must have decided, "OK, so she doesn't want to see us . . . we'll just talk to her." And **talk** they did. I kept hearing the message, "Don't drink," and I would argue with this message.

I've been a therapist in an addiction treatment center, I know how much is too much, and I only drink one glass of wine or one bottle of Heineken a day. That isn't addiction. Still, the message would come, "Don't drink." Still, I would argue.

One night I had a dream, a dream that would make Dicken's *Christmas Carol* look like a scene from *Bambi*. In the dream were two "beings" that stood on either side of me and walked me through my life, beginning, of all places, in the doctor's office. Each place they took me to I was asleep; I couldn't keep my eyes open, especially my left eye, which in ancient literature is the eye to the soul.

The last place I ended up was in was a tall building in front of the elevators, which, by the way, only went to floor two and floor six. Remember Ram Dass and the channels which we operate on? Channel one is our physical body; channel two our personality; channel three new age: libra, pisces rising; channel four, we look into a mirror and there is a multitude of reflections looking back at us; channel five, we look at another individual and that same someone is looking back at us; and channel six is the nothingness from which we came. This elevator only went to floor two (personality) and six (the ultimate). I couldn't make it to floor two because I was asleep.

I awoke the next morning and said, "All right, I won't drink. But you had better show me something." I was always trying to make deals, and my guardians let me think that I was striking deals with the universe.

The following weekend I was giving a dinner party. While sitting at the dinner table listening to a conversation about medical insurance, zoning problems, and which diamond necklace to purchase, I realized how very bored I was and how much I would like a nice glass of wine. In fact, I resented the fact that these individuals were drinking my wine while I was sitting there wishing for a way to escape. I suddenly looked out of my dining room, down the hall, and I saw the eight-foot-tall being with long grey robes cross the hall. "Oh, my God, this is what I've been missing!" I later realized I would see the shadow of this being on the walls and in other places where there was nothing else that could make the shadow.

It was during this same period of initial psychic awareness that my inner voice kept pulling me back to Georgia, the home of my father. For some strange reason I felt the need to find the "Native American" in our family. I was certain that somewhere along the line someone had been married to a Native American. I had cousins that looked like full-blooded Cherokees, and when my father moved to North Carolina, he was good friends with Chief Walking Stick, who was at that time the Chief of the Eastern Band of the Cherokee.

It has been said that once you step out onto the path of seeking your spiritual self you travel a lot, to distant and near places, and you meet the most interesting individuals. I thought of this as I took three days' leave from work and stepped onto a plane headed for a place I had not visited in seventeen years. I arrived to find wonderful, friendly cousins, but only one who would admit to the fact that she thought she had heard my grandmother speak of an "Indian" in the family. Interestingly, I discovered that there was a

Native American burial ground on the family property that was well maintained. My only family connection to the genetic lineage of my father's family, his eldest sister, for reasons of her own, swore that there were no Native Americans in the family despite her three children's black, straight hair, high cheekbones, and dark eyes. While my visit did not turn up any factual evidence of a Native American heritage, I did discover that the family came from Pike County, Louisiana (Cajun?), and I heard the old ghost stories about the family home which I had heard as a child.

For my return to Virginia, I had booked the same flight back as I had coming down. I knew that I remained on the airplane while it made one brief stop in North Carolina. As I sat on the plane waiting for us to take off, I began to hear a voice tell me, "You're on the wrong plane."

"I'm not on the wrong plane. They checked my ticket, this is the same flight I took down; I am on the right plane."

"You're on the wrong plane."

The door closed and we prepared for take off. There were only six of us on the plane, as it was midweek and not many people travel from Augusta to Virginia mid-week. All at once I looked up to see the most handsome man standing by my seat smiling at me. I immediately felt that I was looking at a physician, but I couldn't be certain of his nationality. He had dark hair, intense blue eyes and a wonderful smile. "Pardon me miss, but you are sitting in my seat."

"No, I'm certain I'm in the correct seat." Actually, what difference would it make? "The plane has lots of empty seats," I thought.

I pulled out my ticket, and discovered that I was on

the wrong plane. I just had time to get off, or I would have ended up much further north than was my intention. As I started to get off the plane, I turned to tell the man that I was in his seat and he could move. He wasn't on the plane. The other original five people were still on the airplane and that was *all* that were there. My mysterious physician was nowhere to be seen. Was he my guardian, taking care of me because I wouldn't listen? Or was he a future soulmate, someone out of time and space directing me to pay attention?

When I began trying to hear my inner voice, I had a lot of help. It was clear I didn't pay attention very well! My contact with my inner guidance (or outer guidance, as the case may be) began to become more subtle as I learned to listen. The dramatic events became less and less frequent, the inner voice more prominent. For instance, one morning I had finished a long jog and was getting ready to clean up and go lead a workshop. My husband had requested that I drop off some blueprints for him that morning, as he had out-of-town business. I had forty-five minutes to clean up, deliver the blueprints and get to my workshop location. I jumped into my car, sweaty and smelly, and raced down the street to the office of the architect. I was almost half-way to my destination when I realized, "You have locked yourself out of the house." Which door is open? None. Which window is open? No window. Who else has a key? No one within calling distance. Which window/door do I break to get in?" (All of this was my left brain seeking rational, methodical ways to get into a locked house). It was at this point that the voice in my head said, "If you turn right now you'll run into John (my husband). John had left two hours earlier to go to another city. How could I turn right in the middle of downtown Norfolk, Virginia, and meet him?

I didn't question this information. I turned right, drove a few blocks, and sure enough, I ran into John as he was driving down the street. He had been delayed in leaving town. Coincidence?

I had a similar experience happen when, as was usually the case, I raced out of my home on the way to another city. I reached the end of my driveway and realized I did not have any type of coat. At this particular point in time Virginia had been having a wonderful warm spell in the middle of February. The temperature had been and was predicted to continue to be in the eighties for the next few days. When I realized I didn't have a coat, I thought that a raincoat would be the most practical coat for the occasion. I reached into the closet and pulled out . . . my down parka! I thought, "This is crazy. It's eighty degrees, I am dressed in white linen, the temperature is going to stay in the eighties and I am taking a down parka with me!" But I didn't put it back. I took it to my destination, which was also quite warm—sweater weather at night—and awoke the next morning to an unpredicted and unexpected snow storm. The down parka was the only warm thing I had brought, and luckily so, for I became stranded and had to walk several miles in the snow.

Six: You've Got To Decide Which Way You Are Going To Go.

Even though I was having many wonderful, mystical things happening to me, I was busy furthering my career in the public sector and politics in general. It was an interesting combination, because during the day I would be working with politicians who tried to manipulate the minds of the public, and at night I would be out telling the public to control their own minds, lives, and destinies.

It was while I was attending a political function

that a psychiatrist friend came up and said, "You'll want to meet my neighbor. She's a psychic." I thought, "The last thing I need to meet is another psychic. But when he said "She's eighty years old," I realized I *did* want to meet her. I was sure she had a lot to share.

When I called to make my appointment for a reading, she asked me what I did, and I told her that I was involved in politics but that I was psychic and I enjoyed the mystical side of life.

"You've got to decide which way you are going to go," she said. Those were wise words and exactly what I needed to hear from her. I didn't need a reading to tell me I was psychic or that many changes were taking place in my life. I needed a push from someone who would say, "You have to make a choice. Step out, take a risk, see what happens. It won't be dull!"

The next day I began to set in motion the necessary details to form my own business. I told those I was working with that I wouldn't be taking on any new contracts, that I was going to start consulting in the business world. At this point in time I thought my consulting would be very traditional, based on the knowledge I had acquired both academically and experientially. I was soon to discover that what I thought I was going to consult about and what actually came out of my mouth were two different things. I would go into a setting and say what I thought to be outrageous things about how the mind worked and how we should view life. The amazing thing was that the business community accepted what I said. Certainly something else was helping me in my endeavors . . . something with much more power than I could imagine.

My biggest fear in teaching whole brain thinking was the fact that I would have to learn to relax large groups of people in order to show them how their right hemisphere worked. I had never been comfortable trying to relax anyone, even one person in a private therapy session. How could I possibly think I could relax a large audience, especially one made up of businessmen?

The first workshop I conducted was at a local university and was filled with . . . businessmen and women. I knew I was doing fine until it came time for the relaxation exercise, and then the old fears started to rise. It was then that an interesting thing took place. As I dimmed the lights and turned on the music, I felt an energy come into the room and move behind the audience. When this energy got to my left side I began the exercise. I was extremely calm. It was as though something or someone else were leading the participants . . . exactly where they were supposed to go. After the exercise, I had one woman tell me that she had started to get a migraine, but when I started to talk she felt the tension leave and the beginning of the headache go away. Everyone in the audience seemed to go to a state of utter, complete relaxation. I was amazed.

This type of help has become very normal during the last two years. I always know that an energy will come into the room and lead participants gently into their own state of relaxation. I always know that if I am giving a talk to a specific group of individuals, whether they be architects or physicians, the energy will help me speak specifically to that audience. I will know data and facts that I do not know consciously in this reality, and it will be information that is pertinent to the situation at hand. Even as I sit and write this book I know that things are included that I would not, consciously, have thought to include.

Seven: The Healer and the Mystic

It was after my initial training at Monroe that I

began to psychically "read" anyone who was willing. It was through this practice that I began to learn the difference between my symbols and the symbols that belonged to the individual I was reading. I also began to trust the information I was receiving. If you can verify the answers you receive as soon as possible, you build your confidence in them.

While I was spending all of my spare time "reading" the world, I continued to return to Monroe and play explorer in their lab and moved into doing some interesting remote viewing experiments (remote viewing is the ability to see what is happening at a time and place one has never visited). One day, after being given a series of coordinates and asked to "see" what was there, I saw Sam the Pirate, complete with red mustache and sword. Sam began to tell me information about one of the experimenters in the other room. Essentially, he began to go through her body from head to toe, concluding with, "And this is what she must do if she is to get better." After I came out of the session, I discovered that this information, at least the part that talked about her physical ailments, was correct. She said she could try the remedies he suggested. They made sense to her.

It was later in one of these sessions that I was told I was to work with the healers of the planet. I thought that someone "upstairs" had to be off. What physician did I know that would work with a psychic . . . and one who had absolutely no medical background?

Eight months later I found myself attending a professional meeting and sitting next to a gentleman who introduced himself as a biochemist. It turned out that he was also a physician and is today the primary physician with whom I work. The group of physicians I work with has grown rapidly in number and ranges from internists and surgeons to psychiatrists.

The biochemist, Al, was interested in researching

this phenomenon. What type of information did I receive? Was it accurate, and just as importantly, was it useful? We set up a project to find out. After we conducted our medical readings, often a subject would come back to us to "thank" us for the healing. We would say "thank you," all the while thinking that we weren't healing, we were just scanning the body for useful and helpful information.

One of our readings was for a young woman with temporal lobe epilepsy. After we had given her psychologist the information, it turned out that she wanted to meet with me. I couldn't imagine why. I knew I had said all that there was to say, but I agreed to meet with her at the home of Al and to have her psychologist in attendance. When I met her I saw that she had several serious problems, including a hand that was turning inward and curling up and a speech problem. I remember wondering in my mind just what I was supposed to do, when I heard in my mind, "Heal her."

"You don't understand. I do body scanning and evaluations. I don't *do* healing. Besides, look at her. Her problems are very noticeable. Couldn't you give me someone easy to start with?"
"Heal HER!"

I moved over to the sofa and took her twisted hand in my own. I could feel the energy that she was turning inward on herself.

"Marsha, you are doing this to your body and you have to take control of this energy. No one else can do it for you and you are going to start by healing your hand." I then proceeded to tell her about a past life I saw, where she was a Chinese man who had let his nails grow through his hand in order that he might have control over his life.

"Oh, my gosh," she yelled. "That is the life I saw when I first underwent hypnosis!" She finished the story that I had begun. I felt the energy in the room change and I felt a oneness with this person unlike any I had ever experienced in my life.

Marsha left, her hand still twisted and her speech still slurred. Two weeks later I received a telephone call from Al: "I've got to tell you about Marsha. She was putting a splint on her hand every night in order to keep it from retracting more. She forgot to put the splint on and woke up to find her hand was normal. Not only that, but she doesn't have a speech problem anymore."

One of my most interesting "healing" experiences came when I was with my friend Michael Hutchison (author of *Megabrain*) in New York City. Michael had not been feeling well for several months, and as we strolled around Central Park, I had this strong feeling that I wanted to "heal" him. "Michael, I am going to make you one of the most unusual propositions you may ever receive. I want you to come back to my apartment so that I can heal you."

Michael is truly my brother. I have had some of my most incredible psychic experiences with him, and I have seen past lives where he was my brother and he took care of me. In this life I think it is my turn to take care of him. We returned to the apartment where I was staying, and I remember thinking, "Okay, now what are you going to do? This was your idea, after all."

I asked Michael to lie down. I knew that I wanted to place my hand over his liver and thought, "I'll imagine I am running healing white light here and maybe I'll know what to do next." All at once I felt as if someone or something had thrown a power switch on, and the current began racing through my body with an intensity I had never ever felt. I recall thinking that if it didn't stop soon, I would be so energized I wouldn't be able to sleep, and I wouldn't be able to conduct my workshop the next day.

The next thing I knew I heard a voice say, "That's enough." I felt someone pull a lever and the white light shut off. I immediately fell into a lucid dreamlike state where Michael and I were traveling in a car. When I woke up, Michael had been aware of the whole thing, including the voice that said, "That's enough" and the dream. He had the same dream, and in his dream he even named the dogs which we had picked up by the road, one of which was "Hug A Door."

My only other time of becoming so immersed with this light or energy occurred at the Omega Institute a few years ago. I was in a workshop where we were to imagine ourselves as trees and we were, supposedly, bringing the universal energy from the ground up into our bodies for "grounding." I can't tell you that I believed in that sort of thing. It was one of those instances where it was cold and rainy and my mind was on getting to a warmer space and doing something else. As I stood there in a circle of about twenty individuals, I suddenly became aware that the soles of my feet were becoming hot. I then began to feel the heat move up my legs, and, as it did so, I noticed that everything began to turn golden in color in front of me. As the heat (or energy) moved on up my body, the brightness of the golden color increased and I became physically hotter and hotter. I soon realized that I was unable to see the other people in the circle; all I could see was this very bright, golden light. I began to sweat, and I remember thinking that I had to leave the circle in one way or another. Either I would physically break the chain (we were holding hands) and leave, or I was going to pass out. Just at the point where I felt that I was unable to stand the intensity of the heat and the light any longer, the leader said, "Now bend down to the ground and run the energy back to the source from which it came." I bent over and as I did, I saw a blade of grass that must have been magnified several million times. I could see the intricate workings of the fiber in it, and I could see with great clarity the water droplets on its surface. As soon as I put my head to the ground, the light disappeared and the grass returned to a normal slze.

I have since learned that it is this same golden light that heals, that creates, that helps us be more than our physical bodies. Al and I have witnessed many other healing successes and many attempts at healing where nothing happened. I believe a *Course in Miracles* when it says, "Miracles are natural. It is when they do not occur that something has gone wrong." We both know that it's up to the individual soul to heal its body. I can point out what is causing the situation, tell the person several ways to remedy the situation (which may, in fact, include very traditional medical approaches), but only that soul can heal itself. I also know that added energy can help, e.g., sending white light, visualizing them well, or praying for them.

In section II, "You," I discuss the experiences that have happened to me in terms of their practical application to your life. Intuition *can* be utilized in all aspects of one's life, from personal to business, creativity to health. Let's begin the journey toward seeing with the heart.

You

*It is only
with the heart
that one can
see rightly;
what is essential
is invisible
to the eye.*

Antoine De Saint-Exupery
The Little Prince

Intuitions
Chapter One

Carl Jung once related a story about a conversation with Ochwiay Bianco, then chief of the Pueblo Indians. Bianco when asked, told Jung that his opinion of the white man was not very high because they always seem upset, restless, and looking for something. The result of this is their faces are wrinkled. Not only that, they must be crazy because they think with their heads and it is well known that only crazy people do that. "How do you think?" Jung asked. "Naturally," Bianco replied, "with my heart."

We have the answers; the heart always brings them to us. It is the questions that are difficult. We don't know what we want to know, and we don't know how to ask the question in order to get the answer. In truth, the answers are always right before our nose, ever present.

Gertrude Stein was asked, as she was on her death-bed, if she had found the answers to her questions. "More importantly," she replied, "What is the question?"

We all carry questions around with us, some not fully formulated, many not in our conscious awareness. You may not be happy with your present job, relationship, living environment, etc. Your unhappiness is your heart telling you that you need to make a change; it is time to move on, to grow. All too often we see the door open and realize it represents an answer to an unasked question.

Your heart, or intuition, imagination, creativity, sixth sense, are all the same thing. We just use different names according to the environment we are in. Scientists call it the right hemisphere, Carl Jung called it the "collective unconscious," and Rupert Sheldrake, a present day biologist, calls it "Morphogenetic Resonance."

Intuition is the inner voice, the flow of the universe, energy, the Oversoul, the Higher Self, the I Am presence—in short, it's the sum total of all that we know, all that we can become.

Much has been written on intuition, what it is and what it is not. Discussions abound on whether it exists or doesn't exist. However, despite the many words, clearly there is enough evidence that something exists which provides us information which we have no logical way of knowing; information which, if we act upon it, could be useful and helpful—not only in our everyday lives, but toward our spiritual growth as well.

When I began my workshops, I concentrated on

teaching my students to tap into their psychic/intuitive abilities. Since then, my focus has been to introduce individuals to the "universal energy," the flow of the universe. I tell my students that if we learn to be in touch with that flow, life goes along much more smoothly. It isn't such an effort and battle just to live from day to day. There is a wonderful rhythmic order to things.

As I travel the country teaching people that they are more than their physical bodies, I often use the words psychic and intuition in the same way because they are the same thing. Psychic comes from the Greek word "psyche," meaning soul or spirit. The original definition of a psychiatrist was one who heals the soul, and of psychologist, one who studies the soul. It's time we took the voodoo and mystery out of these words and returned to their original meanings. Every human is "psychic;" that is, we are all spirit.

There are various ways in which we hear "spirit" or receive psychic or intuitive information, the first of these being "physical." Attuned, the physical body is one of the most important means of receiving information that is not apparent. For instance, if you get a headache each time you go to work or when you meet a particular person, it is your body telling you that something is out of sync. Either your work is too stressful and you are creating your own headache in the first example or, in the second instance, the person you are in contact with has a headache, and *you* feel it!

The second type of intuition is "emotional." An example of this would be when you meet an individual who is highly praised by mutual friends, and you aren't able to share those feelings. Until the reasons become apparent, you begin to doubt your own feelings. But when they do, you realize you knew it all the time.

The third type of intuition is "mental" and can be received via dreams or the feeling of *deja vu*, that you have been somewhere before. And it's quite possible that you have, in a dream, visited the very site you found yourself in—years later. Also, using the mental facilities, some people are able to get mental pictures as answers to their intuitive questions.

Since reception of intuitive senses varies from individual to individual, it is important to know how you receive your answers. Some people see pictures, others hear music or voices, and still others just have thoughts pop into their minds—all seemingly from nowhere. Other individuals feel information on their bodies; perhaps they experience a chill when something that is said rings true or is important for them to remember.

I get a pressure on my back if I am checking someone for allergies, or I may actually sneeze if the person is allergic to the substance I am scanning. I also receive chills, and at times my right ear closes if something is being said that I need to pay attention to.

The more we work with our total bodies, the more we can evaluate and use the information which we receive. I feel it is important to ask clear questions, one at a time. Then you should be prepared to see, hear, feel, or experience the answers in the way that your soul speaks to you. When you receive an answer to a question, and we receive answers to our questions all of the time, take time to check the answer. Take it to your heart; how does it feel there? Remember, often we have been carrying a question around with us for months, not realizing that we were asking anything at all. When the answer hits, we have the eureka effect— we know what the question was!

QUESTIONS

Q: How can I tell the difference between "me" and my intuition?

A: Your intuition speaks softly and repeatedly. It isn't judgmental and it doesn't lose patience with giving you the answer again and again, and again. Sometimes it is just a feeling of strong love or uneasiness. The mind, the "chattering mind," uses a lot of shoulds and oughts when it speaks. It is that part of you that tries to make you feel guilty. Guilt is optional, not something we have to do or be.

Q: More than anything else I would like to be psychic, to know the future and to be able to "read" others. How can I?

A: We all know our future because we are busy creating it. Once we become aware of this fact we can work to create what we want and not become engrossed with worrying about what we don't want. As far as being able to "read" others, we do that on a daily basis as well. There are many situations we find ourselves in where we "know" what is taking place but are not at liberty to say what we think or feel. Once you discover that you do know these things, they aren't nearly as interesting. You realize that everyone is alike, on the same path, with the same problems. Being psychic isn't the end result of getting in touch with our intuition. Psychic is only the glitter, there to entice us to see more, lots more. We are trying to get in touch with "spirit" in any way we can; that's what is important.

Q: My intuitive answers seem to come from the center of my chest. When I get a certain feeling there, do I know that a truth is being said or I should follow my feelings?

A: This is your heart bringing you an answer. Know that when your heart brings you an answer, you should follow it. It may be that you find it going in two directions, but then you can go in two directions also. It is more important to open up and experience the knowledge the heart brings, always to do with love, unconditional love, than to shut down and limit life. It may be that if you don't follow your heart and stay only in your head, you will have less emotional response. But then you have to ask yourself, are you making the most of this life if you avoid your feelings and following where your heart leads?

MEDITATION

Sit or lie in a comfortable position with your clothing loose and your shoes off. Watch your breathing; does your breath go deeply into your stomach or does it stop in your chest? Close your eyes and breathe deeply, making sure you take your air all the way down to your lower stomach—about three inches below the navel—the *d'en tien,* as the Chinese call it. After you have watched your breath for a few minutes, begin to notice the thoughts that pop into your head, the pictures that come up, or any other "mental" activity that may be going on.

Observe any feeling that you have *on* your body. Do you have any unusual tingling sensations? Is there any pain or discomfort? Think of someone you don't like. How does your body respond? Do you notice a reaction any particular place on your body? Now think of someone you love or care for. How does your body feel now?

Continue to think of love, letting it flow out into the universal all around you and to all of life. Open your eyes and come back to the present.

EXERCISE

Put on a tape or record of music that has no particular melody, just flowing melody, such as any of the Golden Voyage series (see appendix). Relax and watch the pictures, images, feelings, thoughts, words, or symbols that appear in your mind. Does the music create a picture, a story, or remind you of something in the past? Continue to listen to the music, paying attention to how it affects your physical body as you listen. When the music is over, write down what you saw or felt, along with any other information which came to you during the exercise.

What if you slept?
And what if in your sleep,
you dreamed?
And what if in your dream
you went to heaven and there plucked a
strange and
beautiful flower? And what if,
when you awoke,
you had the flower in your hand? Ah! What
then?

Samuel Taylor Coleridge

INTUITIONS
Seeing With The Heart

Dreams
Chapter Two

In *Dream Game,* Ann Faraday calls dreams "thoughts from the heart." Because I view intuition as information that comes from the heart which you must take back to the heart in order to clarify, I like the concept that dreams also come from the heart. If we view our unconscious as information that comes from our heart, it doesn't become fearful, but rather positive wisdom that helps us move forward in life.

For many years psychologists have tried to fit dreams and the dreamer into a specific mold, which never works. Dreams and their interpretations are as individualistic as the dreamer himself. A more contemporary view of dreams is to have the dreamers make their own interpretation of their dream and to work out the symbology their mind has given to them.

Your mind can only use the symbols and words you are most familiar with, in order to give you a message either about yourself or your life situation. Water in your dreams may not mean the same thing as water in someone else's dream, even though water tends to be a universal symbol for the unconscious and spiritual part of you.

Symbols can be tricky, and you may need to work with your dream over a few days in order to interpret it to your satisfaction. A snake, for example, can mean anything from real snakes in your environment (human or otherwise) to the world of medicine and healing.

An example of a more universal symbol would be a chair. If you are trying to discover the symbology behind the chair, become the chair itself and speak. "I am a chair, people sit on me without any regard for my feelings. I am just a piece of furniture, one that is easily overlooked except when someone wants to use me."

While it may seem as if there are endless possibilities, when you begin recording your dreams and narrowing down your options to specific parameters, the picture gradually comes into focus. These revealing "sign posts" can be used to improve the way you feel about something, hence to improve your life.

The following are some of the most common questions heard concerning dreams:

Q: Why do we dream?
A: Technically, scientists don't know the answer to that. It is known that our REM (rapid eye movement) or dream state is the most important part of our total sleep time. We always dream. On a more personal basis, we dream to get in touch with our heart, our unconscious. Dreams come to tell us something that we don't know about either our

personal life, environment or future. If your dream appears to bring you obvious information, look deeper. There is no need to spend your dream state being told that of which you are already aware.

Q: Why can't I remember my dreams?

A: You have no interest in recalling them. When you decide that you would like to know what is going on in that part of your life, you will send a message to your unconscious mind to begin to help you remember your dreams. Once you have done this, place a pencil and paper or a tape recorder by your bedside. This will serve as a reminder that you are going to recall your dreams and will be writing or telling about them in some manner.

Q: I only remember parts of my dreams; other parts are vague.

A: Upon arising, write down what you do remember and make up the rest. Put down how the dream felt and what you think it was concerning. After this you will find that you will begin to remember a few more details. The habit of recording your dreams will help you to remember them. When you begin to work with your dreams, begin looking for symbols that are consistent and make sense to you. At the end of recording the dream, make a note on what you intend to do about the problem which surfaced in the dream.

Q: There are "dream groups" in which individuals work to help clarify the dreams of others. Are groups useful?

A: Edgar Cayce said that only the dreamer knows the correct meaning of his dream, and it is correct only when it makes sense to him and feels right. In addition, the dream should be consistent with other dreams and move the dreamer forward in life. I think that the dreamer should first make his interpretation of the dream, and then ask others for their insights if need be, but to go to a group solely for the purpose of having them make the interpretation allows the dreamer to become lazy in processing his inner work.

Q: What if after working very hard on a dream I still don't understand it?
A: Ask your higher consciousness for a clarification dream. This is a dream that brings you the same answer in a different way. You can also ask for verification on the way that you interpreted the dream.

Q: Are all dreams the same?
A: Dreams can be classified according to the information which they provide or the feeling they invoke:

Precognitive dreams are dreams which contain information on future events. You may or may not be able to act upon this information and it may or may not concern you. It is possible for a precognitive dream to give you information about someone you barely know.

Symbolic, possibly the most common type of dream, which serves to bring us information from our unconscious to help us move forward.

Lucid, or out-of-body dreams, where the dreamer knows he is dreaming. In the lucid state the dreamer has the option of flying, changing the plot, going to see anyone he desires or to any place he thinks about. Dreams about flying or some mode of transportation should serve as an alert to the dreamer that he has been out of body.

Q: I frequently dream of my husband. Am I really dreaming about him or am I dreaming about the male part of myself?

A: Because you know your husband, the dream is telling you something about him or your relationship to him. When you dream of someone you know, the dream is actually about them. When you dream of a stranger you must look to interpret if the stranger is a part of you of which you are not aware, an actual person you might meet in the future, or something else entirely. If, for example, you dream of a "John Hurt," ask yourself if you actually know a John Hurt. If there is no one in your life with the name of Hurt, ask if someone is hurting you or if you are hurting someone else by your actions. Remember that dreams come to tell us what we don't consciously know, not what we are aware of.

Q: How do I learn to have an out-of-body experience?

A: Every one of us "travels" during our sleep. The trick is to remember that we traveled or to be aware (lucid) at the time we are traveling. Ask your higher self to make you aware of when you travel. It may take a few days or weeks before you begin to be knowledgeable about this state, and you may find that you are aware for only a few minutes, that you only got a passing glimpse of your out-of-body state. As you become more aware of what it feels like to be "out," you can consciously work to be more aware of "getting out," of freeing your astral body from your physical body.

Q: Are there specifics to be included when recording dreams?

A: Yes. Try seeing your dream as a "dream play" and write your notes accordingly. This will help you begin to interpret your dreams more fully and enhance your enjoyment of writing them down.

Consider:

#1 The setting or time and place of the dream and its relevance to the present. Did the dream take place during the Civil War, and did you find yourself in a Confederate hospital? Do you work in the medical profession now? Are you trying, or not trying, to be civil to someone . . . possibly a confederate?

#2 The plot or trigger points. Do you find you are unable to complete a specific task no matter how many times you try? Is the confederate undermining you in some fashion?

#3 The scene. Where does this scene fit in the rest of your dreams, your life? Does the scene change?

#4 Cast of characters. Are they people that you know, love, or are they strangers? How do they relate to you in this scene?

#5 The feeling. How does this dream leave you feeling? After you interpret the dream, you should feel uplifted with new insight. If you don't then you have misinterpreted the dream. Dreams don't come to us to make us unhappy; they come to give us clarity.

#6 Word play. For example, a person named "Rob" could suggest the act of robbing someone or taking something that doesn't belong to you, and the word "gilted" could be masking the word "guilt."

#7 The denouement, the peak of the dream, the incident when the plot matures and reaches its climax. This is the opportunity for the characters to separate themselves from the plot, and the dreamer has the opportunity to see how they react in his "real" life.

Although most people have a favorite or an out-

60

standing dream, my favorite is not one I dreamed myself. It came to me by way of a telephone call from a distant friend who had dreamed of me the night before. I had a vague recollection of having thought (dreamed?) of him as well.

He explained the dream and then named the other leading character.

It was, indeed, someone I knew. But what made the dream so outstanding was the fact that this long and distant friend had never heard of the other person in the dream prior to having the dream.

MEDITATION

Relax in bed with the lights off. Scan your mind and release any worries or thoughts from the day that seem to be hanging on. This can be done by visualizing the problem, seeing it with a perfect ending, surrounding it with a pink bubble, and releasing it to the universe. (See Chapter 10, "Visualization.")

Select an area of your life to which you would like an answer. Frame the question as simply and as clearly as you can, e.g. "Should I consider the new job that is opening at work?" Ask your heart to bring you an answer. Be sure that you have a note pad and pencil next to your bed in order to record your dreams when you awaken.

During the day, ask yourself if you are dreaming. According to Stephen LeBerge *(Lucid Dreaming)*, this will help you be aware of when you are dreaming at night and make it easier for you to have a lucid dream.

Actively create a dream. Write down a dream that you would like to have occur. Remember to put it in color and add all of the details you would like to see happen, including people, places and things. When you have finished recording the dream, fold the paper toward you three times and place it in a safe, loving space. Wait, and see what happens.

Go confidently in the direction of your dreams!
Live the life you've imagined.
As you simplify your life,
the laws of the universe
will be simpler;
Solitude will not be solitude,
poverty will not be poverty,
nor weakness weakness.

Henry David Thoreau

INTUITIONS
Seeing With The Heart

Life/Career
Chapter Three

What shall I do with the rest of my life is probably one of the most common questions put to a psychic. Ironically, this question is usually not asked by the high school or college graduate, but by individuals reaching their mid-thirties or beyond, ready to take a hard look at why they are where they are. There is a strong desire to know whether or not we are doing whatever it is that we came to do.

Our purpose in life changes as we move through the learning that is taking place on a soul level. We are all here to learn, to wake up, to remember that which we already know. In fact, we work hard at not remembering all that we know, just so we can learn the lessons we have created for ourselves in any one lifetime.

When we are born, and before our educational system begins to educate us in the ways of rational, analytical thinking, we know who we are and why we are here. By the time we reach the end of the first grade, we have begun to forget our primary purpose and have taken on the role of student of the left brain hemisphere and its thinking. Originally, the left brain was simply a filter, a tool for helping the right hemisphere put out what it was receiving. Through years of inaccurate thinking and pressure, the left brain began to take on a dominant role, and to speak for the ego, as though it were the wisdom within.

It is little wonder that the question of career and job changes comes up as fequently as it does. Before anyone asks the question of whether or not to change jobs, they should see why they are asking the question in the first place. If your mind gives you a question, or begins to have you ponder a situation, you can be certain that the answer is already right before you, and in all probability the answer is yes. If the energy that you are feeling is content with everything else that is going on in your life, the question of change would not arise in the first place.

Regardless of how some people may try to disguise it, they are not happy and they are unable to realize this fact because they are locked into a thought system which limits their perspective and aspirations. Know that your soul is constantly urging you, very quietly, to wake up, to know who you are and to be in harmony with its inner urging.

QUESTIONS

Q: I feel as though I am constantly swimming upstream. Sometimes I think I should go in a different direction, but I don't know where to go and I've put so much work into being where I am. What should I do?

A: When we are in harmony with our inner voice and the natural flow of the universe, doors open easily for us. When a door closes, the universe is telling us to look in another direction, that our energy is not harmonious with this particular path. When we find we are swimming upstream, we are going against the natural flow. We can make life difficult or we can make it easy. It's our choice. It doesn't have to be difficult in order for us to learn and to be able to help others.

Q: I am presently in medical school, working very hard. Sometimes I wonder if I should have to spend so much of my lifetime giving up my private life and moments in order to be a healer. Couldn't this be easier?

A: Zen masters have taught us that we have to put forth the energy in order to have that which we wish to take place happen. There is a difference between swimming upstream, going against the flow, and working hard to achieve a goal. One lifetime is but a blink of an eye in the total picture of our developing soul. You have probably spent many lifetimes learning the art of healing in one way or another and now you are working to re-member it. Don't discount the academic information you are acquiring now. After all, at some point it came from someone's intuition.

Q: Does it matter what I do for a career? Isn't it true that we all get to the same place anyway? I could work or not work and still get there.

A: It is true that ultimately we all get to the same point. However, in life it is the journey, not the destination that counts. You can make the journey an interesting one or one that is boring. As you make your journey interesting, you create learning situations for yourself that help your soul to grow and to be nourished. It doesn't matter how you make the journey, but it would be nice if you took time to smell the roses along the way.

Q: What is my purpose of being here this time around?

A: All souls have the same purpose—to learn, and to remember the source from which they came. So many individuals think that they have to have a lofty purpose, to save the world, not realizing that saving the world begins with them . . . *inside*. They are so busy looking outside of themselves for that purpose, they fail to learn who they really are until it is too late. It is important to work in changing the self, not the world. Imposing your own answers on the world is not allowing others to follow their own goals, to march to their own drummer. No matter how insignificant you may think your role on this planet is, know that you would be sorely missed if you were not here. No other soul can fill your space. It is not the job you are doing, but the energy you bring to the planet.

Q: I feel as though I should make a move to another city in order to further my career, but I seem to block when it comes to knowing exactly where to go.

A: The universe gives us signs and guideposts that tell us we are on the right path and going in the right direction. For example, I had known for three years that I was going to be moving from Norfolk, Virginia, early in 1987, but I didn't know where. Last fall, following a workshop in Pennsylvania, one of the participants approached me and told me that she had a feeling I was going to move to Boston.

What followed was a series of "signs," e.g., the few times I turned on the T.V., either the Boston

Celtics were playing or it was the Public Broadcasting System flashing BOSTON across the screen. On more than one occasion, I would be flying across country and discover that I was sitting next to someone from Boston on the airplane. Just when I was beginning to feel that I was making all of this up, I looked up (I was driving around Virginia) and I was following a car that had a Boston University sticker on it.

These are important signs in life and it is important to notice them. The universe gives us "totems" for a reason—to give us concrete signs, which is what our left brain likes, that we are on the right path. If you are unclear about what to do, ask for a sign. It will be given to you.

Once I made my move to New England, other positive affirmations followed. I began to book more seminars and workshops, and opportunities opened up at a hospital for working with staff and patients. I was also able to continue in more detail my research with Dr. Albert Dahlberg of Brown University. We are exploring the connection between intuitive medical information and traditional medical information in an effort to bring the two together in a constructive manner.

Q: How can I trust what I am feeling?
A: You have to act on the information which you receive. Watch for the totem signs and doors to open. If they open easily, the chances are good that you are on the right path; if they open with difficulty or slam shut, perhaps you are being told to look elsewhere.

Q: How will I know when to quit?
A: When things are so difficult that it is virtually impossible to accomplish anything, and you feel that you take two steps backward for each step you

take forward, look in another direction. Life does not have to be difficult. Making it less so may be as easy as letting go of a difficult or impossible goal. Who set the goal in the first place? Was it your original goal or that of your parents or someone else in authority? Perhaps it was a goal you set because of shoulds and oughts. Letting go will free you to move to a higher purpose which may presently be masked by excessive energy in the wrong direction. Just remember when you are on the right path, things become easy. The exception to this rule is the person who makes it to where he wants to be in spite of hard times. Consider, it may not have had to be via "hard times." Could it be he created the hard times because his belief system said only through hard work do we reach our goals?

Q: How do I know I have made the right choice?

A: It will feel right when you align the mental picture or thought of what you have decided upon with the feeling you get from your heart. Put yourself in a meditative state and relax. Ask your highest source of information for guidance and state verbally or mentally what you have decided to do. Then wait and see how it feels on your body. The correct answer will balance with the heart chakra. You will feel a warmth and centeredness there and know yours was the correct choice. If, on the other hand, you feel nervous or anxious then substitute your choice with other alternative choices. See which one feels the most comfortable on your body.

Q: Do the right choices always reap rewards?

A: Yes. One way or another rewards manifest themselves in positive ways: contentment with ourselves, knowing we are doing what our souls want us to be doing, and doing something because it is what *we* want to do and not something others expect of us.

Q: There is a job I would like to have, but someone else is in the position. I don't want to do anything harmful to them, yet I can't see anything else I would rather do.

A: One of the major problems with creating our life and career is to think that there is only one of anything. We forget that it is an abundant universe and there is plenty for all . . . even jobs. You can visualize your ideal job, complete with salary and working conditions, release that vision and know that it, or something better, will manifest in your life. By visualizing what you wish to create in your life, you don't take away from someone else. Their soul/spirit is constantly manifesting for them as well. It is possible that the person in the job you want will be promoted or take a higher paying job elsewhere. As long as you visualize for the good of all you don't need to be worried. You do not have the power to manipulate another's soul, just your perception and creation of reality.

Q: I don't know what I want. Where do I start?

A: There are many individuals in this world who do not know what they want. Whenever I get a clear picture of what I want, it is there, almost immediately. However, getting to this clarity may mean weeks or months of unconscious processing as to what it is I want.

One way to start to see what you want is to relax and visualize what you see yourself doing five, ten years from now. Look at or feel the picture in great detail; who is with you, where are you, what are you doing as a career, are you happy? If you are not happy, then look to see how you would change the picture and make that change in your mind. Be sure to put yourself in the picture.

After you have this image of yourself in the future, sit down with a pencil and paper and write out short-term goals (the next year), mid-term goals (the next five years) and long-term goals (the next ten years). Be sure to make your goals reasonable and obtainable. For instance, don't have your goal be to lose one hundred pounds in one month. This is not only not realistic, it is not healthy.

If, for some reason, you don't obtain one of your goals, don't judge yourself as having failed. Simply know that your goal has changed and you are not putting the energy into it that you were initially. Goals, like everything else in life, need to be flexible and able to flow with the universal energy.

Q: I don't feel that I am free to run my own life. I have too many demands made on me that I have to meet.

A: No matter how you frame the question, you are always responsible for your own life and for the demands made upon you. If you feel others take advantage of you then you are allowing them to do so. Remember, you create your own reality and you attract to you as you think. If you don't feel that you are a free spirit and able to control your life, start asking for help from your highest source of information and know that it will come.

MEDITATION

Asking life questions is probably one of the most difficult areas to focus on and to see clearly. It is important to take a sufficient amount of time, thirty minutes or so, to relax before you begin to ask your source for information about you and your future.

After you are relaxed, ask yourself the following questions:

Am I happy?

If not, what is keeping me from being happy?

What am I looking for?

What about my life/career do I like?

When I look back on my life from the age of 100, what will I like about it?

When I look back on my life from the age of 100, what would I like to change?

Thank your higher self for this information. Request that you be given "guideposts" that you are going in the right direction; then watch for them!

The fact that the mind rules the body is, in spite of its neglect by biology and medicine, the most fundamental fact which we know about the process of life.

Franz Alexander, M.D.

We must remove the word "impossible" from our vocabulary. As David Ben-Gurion once observed in another context, "Anyone who doesn't believe in miracles is not a realist." Moreover, when we see how terms like "spontaneous remission" or "miracle" mislead and confuse us, then we will learn. Such terms imply that the patient must be lucky to be cured, but the healings occur through hard work. They are not acts of God. Remember that one generation's miracle may be another's scientific fact. Do not close your eyes to acts or events that are not always measurable. They happen by means of an inner energy available to all of us. That's why I prefer term like "creative" or "self-induced" healing, which emphasize the patient's active role.

Bernie S. Siegel, M.D.
Love, Medicine and Miracles

Health
Chapter Four

Robbie Gass once put out a flyer that began, "You will receive a body. You may like it or hate it, but it will be yours for the entire period this time around." All too often the concept of taking care of the body is forgotten, put on hold for another day, or ignored completely with the hope that the body will take care of itself. It does—perhaps not the way we would like for it to take care of itself—but it does form itself according to our thoughts and thinking patterns.

Of all of the realities that your belief system creates, your physical well-being is perhaps the most important. If you are not healthy in body, how can you begin to believe that you can create abundance and happiness in your life? Western society's belief in physicians is overwhelming. The belief systems between patient and doctor affect not only the ultimate recovery of the patient, but the belief in the ability of one's body to heal itself.

It has been my experience in working with physicians, as we apply non-traditional intuitive approaches to medicine, that it is about five years after graduating from medical school that they begin to realize they don't have all of the answers. Patients that should get better die, and patients that don't have a chance of living live. What happens? Are these miracles? Or just tomorrow's science made known today? It is my feeling that in ten years the work we are researching with the mind/ body relationship will be common knowledge, the way things work naturally.

The first step on the road to a healthy body is the awareness that your thoughts are creating your physical body. Worries that you carry around with you express themselves in wrinkles and frown lines, burdens or weights show up as backaches, and people or problems you can't stomach become ulcers, gastritis, colitis.

The body is a wonderful barometer not only of what is going on within your own mind, but around you in your environment. It will quickly inform you it needs rest, food (carbohydrates or protein) or exercise. You intuitively know if you have received too much sun, or if you should consult a physician about some problem that is worrying you.

Instantly, when you are injured, you know if you have broken a bone, or if it is just a superficial injury, such as a sprain. Because you know these things doesn't mean that you pay attention to them. In this country we think if we aren't active then we aren't being productive, and being productive may mean continuing to work even when we don't feel like it.

If we push our bodies to the limit, e.g., working

long hours when our intuition tells us to rest, drinking coffee to keep going, we are sending the body a message that it will have to yell loudly in order for us to pay attention. Loudly may be too late. It could mean hospitalization or some other serious illness.

The more medical readings I conduct, the more aware I am of our emotional state and its reaction on the body. What follows are some common physical illnesses and the emotion behind the illness or pain.

Backache: carrying a burden, more reponsibility than need be. Sharp back pains indicate someone is stabbing you in the back.

Stomach pain, ulcers: something that you can't "stomach."

Extremities: inability to move forward, to make change.

Throat: lack of communication, something isn't being said.

Vision: not seeing clearly, avoiding intuition.

Hearing: not paying attention to one's inner voice.

Heart: inability to express love.

Cold: need to nourish oneself, to rest, to regroup.

Cancer: emotions are bottled up inside, need to be expressed.

Q: If meditation is as important as people say it is, then why do I have to exercise or eat properly? It seems I should be able to do whatever I want, meditate, and be healthy.

A: We are here in human form and it is important to take care of the form. The form we chose was created in order to learn, and learning does not take place without the active movement of energy. The body was meant to work, to be in motion, to be enjoyed. Meditation can do many things and there certainly are examples of yogis who only meditated and lived to ripe old ages. You, however, are not a yogi; you are someone living in the stress-induced environment of western society. You need to exercise and eat properly.

Q: You mention eat properly. Doesn't what I "eat" buy into my belief system? If I think it is good for me then it is, and if I think it is bad then it will do harm?

A: Basically yes. The problem is that we have all been educated that the only way to be healthy is to eat three well-balanced meals a day. We are slowly changing our beliefs to read, "It is better to eat several small meals" and "red meat is not necessarily good for you." The fitness craze sweeping the country has substituted one belief system for another, all concerned with what we put into our mouths. Technically you might be able to eat anything you desired with no ill effect—it all turns to carbohydrate to be burned in the end—but mentally it would be difficult for you to break away from years of programming about nutrition.

Q: Is there a natural way to slow down the aging process?

A: Individuals I know that seem to have "slowed" the aging process never think about how old they are. In fact, if asked, they may have to do a bit of calculation; it just isn't something that concerns them. Getting older is a fact of life, but it doesn't mean that our bodies have to fall apart on us or that we have to look our age.

Q: I am afraid that if I get in touch with my higher self I will know when I am going to die, and that scares me.

A: We all know when we are going to die. It is when death rides on our left shoulder, our future, that we can begin to learn to live. It is good to be aware of when you are "scripting" your death, however. You may want to change it. We usually "script" our death according to the death of the parent of our same sex. They are our role model and their illnesses and death are the only model we have for getting out of this reality. Look to see what age you think you are going to die. As you get older you may discover that you have chosen an age that is actually quite young. Change it. By being aware of how we think we are going to die, or the scripting we are placing ourselves in, we can sort out irrational fears and get in touch with our inner voice that has no fear of death.

Q: Just how do we listen to our bodies?
A: Our body is a barometer. The headache tells us more than just that we are having a withdrawal from caffeine. It tells us we don't like our work situation, someone we are with, etc. We have to learn to read these clues. Your neck pain may be telling you that a person or situation is a "pain in the neck."

Also, as you begin to open up spiritually, you become sensitive to the pain of others. In effect, you become a sponge and soak up all information, pain, and feelings around you. The next time you experience a headache ask yourself, "What's the matter with my head?" If it's your headache, your head will hurt more, if it isn't your headache, if it belongs to someone else, it will go away.

MEDITATION

Relax in a favorite chair or place. Loosen your clothing and put your feet up. Notice if any part of your body is uncomfortable and adjust yourself so that it doesn't bother you. Try not to think of problems or solutions. Take a deep breath. As you inhale, visualize a warm white light flowing down from the top of your head, moving slowly through your body and out the soles of your feet. Imagine that everything that you need and desire is flowing to you as you breathe in. As you exhale, draw the white light up the outside of your body until it reaches the top of your head and begins to circulate around and down. Exhale out all of the things that you don't feel are beneficial to you: poor health, jealousy, anxiety, poverty.

After you have done this for a few minutes, visualize your physical body. If you can't do this at first, then sense it, touching that portion of yourself which may ache or be experiencing pain or discomfort.

Next, direct the white light to that portion of your body you feel needs healing. Feel the warmth and intensity of the light as it moves in and through this area. Know that you and the universal source of energy, of which you are a part, are healing your body, restoring it to perfection.

Another shift I see that really impresses me is a new respectability for intuition in corporate settings. Now people are willing to say, "I just feel this is going to work."

John Naisbitt, *Megatrends*

Business Decisions
Chapter Five

The use of the "mind" is playing a more prominent role in business management and decisions today than ever before. Some feel that in fifteen years using intuition to make business decisions will be perfectly normal, as right-brain thinking gains more prestige due to competitive demands placed on this country from markets such as Japan, where intuition in the workplace has brought considerable profit, and by American blue-chip companies' acceptance of the approach. Among the forerunners in this mental revolution are companies such as Arco, Dow Corning, IBM, Kodak, etc.

What is happening because of the mental revolution is that more and more executives at the top are

81

realizing that making decisions is not a function exclusively of the analytical left brain; it is an integration of both the left and the intuitive right. Simply stated, right brain management is allowing the intuitive, creative side of the brain to have a voice in making decisions in tandem with the analytical left side. In the corporate world this theory is referred to as whole brain thinking.

The word used is "hunch" and it has been used by many decision-making executives who frequently make decisions against the statistics in front of them, preferring to rely on that "gut" feeling, and many times to their benefit. The history of business is replete with data suggesting that some who totally relied on available information and research made the wrong decisions based on those findings. One recent example was Coca-Cola's decision to market a new formula for "Coke."

Of course, doing "homework" continues to be necessary before making financial or business decisions. However, information which is assessed by the left brain tends to be more profitable when intergrated with input from the right brain.

As whole brain thinking gains respectability, more big corporations are exposing their CEOs to seminars on the subject and are finding the results beneficial in marketing, selecting personnel, predicting future trends, and purchasing equipment.

Since whole brain thinking is a new-age concept, many feel awkward when asking for help and frequently preface their questions concerning right brain thinking with, "I know this is a dumb question, but...," because they feel they should already have the analytical or business acumen to know the answer.

Below are a sampling of some of the more general questions asked at whole brain seminars:

Q: How will I know when it's the right time to buy property?

A: Owning property starts with a seed planted in the subconscious, which, if nurtured, will grow until it matures into a full feeling that you want to own something that is part of the earth. Just as we put out thoughts that draw certain people to us, so it is with home ownership. Perhaps it will begin by turning into a wrong street, only to find the home of your dreams with a "For Sale" sign on the lawn.

Q: How do I tell when it's the "right" time to begin a business venture?

A: If it feels right, go for it. But, if on the other hand, you feel nervous, anxious or unsure and experience a certain tightness in your head when you think about it, it is best to postpone your decisions until these uneasy feelings leave.

Begin by assessing your emotions, center on yourself by relaxing and moving inward. The morning hours may be best for this exercise, for your activity is at its lowest point and your mind shouldn't be crowded with the activities of the day.

One final note, and this is to those who may wish to speculate more liberally. It is possible to control certain fundamentals of our environment, which means it is possible to be a wild card winner. A case in point is Ray Kroc who purchased the McDonald hamburger chain, going against the advice of his lawyer and financial advisor.

The payoff: The Golden Arches!

EXERCISE

For problem solving:
Pull all available data together and review as you would for any type of decision. Put the data aside and

go for a walk, play tennis, have a cup of coffee. Wait for the insight to "pop" into your mind.

Prior to going to sleep put the "problem" in the hands of your higher self and ask that you be given a dream with the information you need. Write down your dream upon awakening.

Relax in a sitting or reclining state. Place the problem before you in your mind and ask yourself for a solution. When you sense a picture, word, or thought or other type of information see how it feels on your body. Look to your heart chakra . . . is there a centeredness there? A feeling of well-being when you get the answer? Or, are you anxious, unclear? If the latter is the case, take the question back to your higher self and keep looking for the solution that feels most comfortable on your physical body and your heart chakra.

VISUALIZATIONS

For an important meeting:

Relax, allow white light to flow throughout your body, starting with your head and working its way down to your feet. Imagine that you are in the meeting room with the person or persons you will be with. See everyone, including yourself, in great clarity. Have the situation take place exactly as you would like to see it, include a feeling of warmth, love, and friendliness as you do this. Surround this picture with a pink balloon, release it, and know that this, or something better, will manifest for you.

When love beckons to you, follow him,
Though his ways are hard and steep.
And when his wings enfold you, yield to him,
Though the sword hidden among his
pinions may wound you.
And when he speaks to you, believe in him,
Though his voice may shatter your dreams
as the north winds lays waste the garden.

For even as love crowns you so shall he
crucify you. Even as he is for your growth
so he is for your pruning.
Even as he ascends to your height and
caresses your tenderest branches that
quiver in the sun,
So shall he descend to your roots and
shake them in their clinging to the earth.

Like sheaves of corn he gathers you
unto himself.
He threshes you to make you naked.
He shifts you to free you from your husks.
He grinds you to whiteness.
He kneads you until you are pliant;
And then he assigns you to his sacred
fire, that you may become sacred bread for
God's sacred feast.
All these things shall love do unto you
that you may know the secrets of your heart,
and in that knowledge become a fragment of
Life's heart.

Kahlil Gibran, *The Prophet*

Relationships
Chapter Six

Relationships may be one of our most difficult lessons in any one lifetime. How to love, how to let go, how to find that special someone we feel is out there. Regrettably, few people listen to the resonance from within themselves which can help them find not only where they belong, but with whom they belong (or when they're with the wrong person).

As difficult as the advice may be to someone who feels that they are "destined" to be alone, begin to *enjoy* being alone with yourself. Find out who you are, treat yourself with special care; in short, use the time to learn to love yourself.

At the same time, if you truly desire a relationship, affirm daily that you are attracting to you the perfect mate; "I am now attracting the most perfect relationship."

Recognize the relationship when it presents itself. Know that you become what you think of, and begin to create your life from your thoughts. In order to have the relationship that is the most perfect for you at this point in time, it is important to know that the perfect partner is coming to you, you have earned this relationship, you deserve it, and it is your birthright.

QUESTIONS

Q: How do I know when a relationship is right for me?

A: Listen to your inner voice. How do you feel when you are with this person? Is it all sexual attraction or is there more? Is there an attraction you can't quite label? Know that if the only qualities you are attracted to in this individual are based on some type of emotional or financial insecurity within yourself the relationship is in trouble from the very beginning. It is easy to let our logical brain tell us this is the perfect relationship because of the material things it offers, but we must be willing to look at our "gut" feelings when evaluating the total picture.

Q: Does everyone have a soulmate or twin soul?

A: Yes, but soulmates and twin souls are separate things. Before we incarnated on this plane we were whole entities, both male and female. When we chose to incarnate, we split into either a dominate male or dominate female in order to learn life's lessons from that viewpoint. This other half of us is our exact opposite, our twin soul. We are always learning the lessons that he or she is learning. As we near that time in our lifetimes when most of our learning on this plane is complete, we are drawn to our twin in order to work out the differences we have created.

Q: You say differences. Does this mean that the relationship is not always perfect?

A: That's exactly what it means. You are working through the problems of your other self, the opposite of you. It may be difficult, but extremely satisfying as you clear away the garbage you have created throughout many lifetimes.

Q: Can you do this without arguments or disagreements?

A: Probably not. That would be denying the humanness of ourselves. Underneath the disagreements lies an intense love that knows we are trying to be clear, to be one.

Q: Is it possible that we won't meet our twin soul?

A: You may not meet your twin if you have a number of lifetimes of work to be as complete as you can. We have to be as whole in ourselves, as complete in ourselves as we possibly can be, before we meet our twin. When we are in that space we can't help but attract each other. It's our destiny.

Q: That explains twin souls, but what about soulmates? We hear a lot about soulmates these days.

A: Soulmates are souls we have been with through many lifetimes; ones we have married frequently, ones who have been our business partners, ones with whom we have both created and worked through karma.

Q: You say this as though we have many soulmates.

A: We do. That's why there are any number of individuals we can fall in love with and be happy with, at least until we have worked through the reason of our being together.

Q: Why do people fall "out of love?"

A: It's not falling out of love, it's finishing our roles together. Relationships, like everything else, move to a rhythm, a cycle. Once we are in touch with this rhythm, we know when it is time to follow the energy to the next stage in our life.

Q: Are you saying that separation and divorce shouldn't be seen as such a traumatic and negative thing?

A: That's exactly what I'm saying. As you may know, I recently ended a long-term relationship. We had come together during college and supported each other both financially and emotionally. That was our role for that point in time. As we changed, our needs and concepts of what relationships should be changed. I realized that my husband was really my brother and that was the type of love I felt for him. I don't love him any less after this realization, but I recognize he isn't the person at this point in my life who can help me grow the most. Nor am I the person who can help him grow from now on.

Q: How did you come to this realization?

A: I realized there was something missing in the relationship, something I could not name, but something I was looking for . . . had, in fact, been looking for all of my life.

Q: What do you think it was?

A: My twin soul.

Q: Have you met your twin soul?

A: Yes.

Q: How do you know?

A: I just *know*.

Q: Why do some people settle for less than a twin, or soulmate?

A: They don't know how to "trust" that the universe always provides and that everything is on schedule. We have to learn to trust and to be patient. Many individuals start counting their chronological age; "I'm 34, if I don't marry now I never will, or I'll never have a family," etc.

Q: Do you think people know that they are settling for less?

A: Oh, yes. Many friends, now divorced, have said that on their wedding day they knew it wouldn't last. They knew they were marrying the "wrong" person. They had deliberately blocked their inner voice. They equated being empty and unfulfilled with being alone. If only they had realized that by learning to love and accept themselves for the soul they really are, they would draw their true partner to them.

Q: What advice would you give to someone waiting for their life's partner?

A: The advice given by a good friend who once reminded me that, "Relationships are like roses. You have to let them unfold naturally. You don't try to pry them open."

EXERCISE (for present relationship)

Sit quietly, take a deep breath, close out the external and focus your thoughts inward. Relax and ask yourself, one question at a time:

- How did you feel when you first met your current love?
- Was it strictly a physical attraction or was there more to it?
- Were you attracted to this person by some

intangible magical aspect?
- Did you feel you had known this person before?
- How do you feel about him/her now?
- How does he/she feel about you?
- Is this the person you are truly supposed to be with?
- Do you still feel there is someone else out there?
- Do you want to be with him/her for the rest of your life?
- Could you spend days/weeks with him or her, without a physical relationship, and be content and happy?
- Are the two of you seldom alone? Is it frequently necessary to be part of a crowd? Can you talk at a deep level about yourself, your desires, fears, etc, or do you edit what you say, fearing your partner won't understand, won't be interested?
- How do you feel when together? Are you peaceful, contented or are you anxious to keep moving?
- Do you think something is missing in this relationship?

The above list may be incomplete. You may have personal questions of a specific nature which may need to be addressed. These should be added to the list and answered honestly and as intuitively as possible. Go with the first answer that pops into your mind. Don't discount it or rationalize it away.

EXERCISE

Sit or lie in a relaxed position. Imagine the white light is coming down from the universe and flowing through your head down to your feet, then circulating around to your head again. Let the white light continue to flow in this manner for a few minutes. Now ask that your higher self, or the highest source of information that you contact, be present. Affirm to this source and to the universe that you are ready for your heart chakra to open. You are now ready to give and receive love.

In your mind's eye see the white light focusing on your heart area and then moving out into the universe.

Affirm "My soul mate (or twin soul) is coming to me. I am love and I attract love to me. My soul mate is love and is attracted to me. My soul mate is coming to me now."

Use the term soul mate or twin soul, depending on what your intuition tells you to use. You will attract the one that is most perfect for you at this point in time.

Thank the universe for its help and come back to the present, knowing that your perfect relationship is making its way to you.

Remember, when you have attracted that special someone to you, relationships are like roses . . . you must let them unfold, naturally.

It's the heart afraid of breaking
That never learns to dance.
It's the dream afraid of waking
That never takes the chance.
It's the one who won't be taken
Who cannot seem to give,
And the soul afraid of dying
That never learns to live.

Fear
Chapter Seven

Fear is a universal emotion and can be ranked next to love and hate in intensity. It is possible that we do more things out of fear than from any other emotion that we experience.

Our society has raised us in a system of fear: fear of God, fear of failure, fear of success. From early on religion taught us to fear that which we didn't know, in short, to fear the "I Am" part of ourselves. By being taught fear, and the fact that our lives are beyond our control, we have been limited in our understanding of how the universe works. There is magic out there, and we create it every moment of our lives.

The key to conquering our fears is to become aware that the universe is ordered and magical with a source of intelligence that helps us in times of need and/or trouble. Within this order is the fact that everything is on schedule, there are no accidents. What we give rise to as fear is just one more lesson that we have created in order to learn while we are here. Hopefully, we learn our lessons as they are presented in order not to have to repeat the same lesson lifetime after lifetime. All of life contains lessons; otherwise you wouldn't be here.

QUESTIONS

Q: Why am I so afraid to admit that I am psychic, or to get in touch with my psychic abilities?

A: Two reasons: you have been brought up in a society where our religious institutions teach us that the unknown is dark and evil, that you have no control over your life. No doubt you have been told, or have read somewhere, that psychic or metaphysical awareness is the work of the devil. The part of you that doesn't trust yourself believes some of this. The other part of this answer is that, perhaps, you have had a past life where you died for expressing what you believed in, for knowing there was more out there. There is a part of you that doesn't want to repeat that experience.

I went through a similar experience when I was first developing my psychic awareness. I found I was afraid to admit I was psychic and would frequently do everything I could to block the experiences. One evening I had an out-of-body experience and past life regression (unplanned) simultaneously, where I became myself burning and dying as a witch. I knew I had red hair and green eyes, and I could see the faces of the onlookers as I burned. After that I thought, "So what's the worst thing that can happen to me for admitting that I am psychic? I die. When we realize we come back again, and again, it isn't so frightening.

Q: Am I afraid of dying?

A: At some time in their lives, everyone is afraid of dying. They don't know what is out there, they think of missing those they love, and of all the things they thought they needed to accomplish. When we choose to move on to another reality, we can be assured that we have completed our purpose for this time around. If you're still here you have more work to do. Individuals terminally ill usually move past their fears of death. They know there is more. Many report of seeing guardian angels by their beds and in their dreams. These angels are there to help make the journey easy. As the lyric from "The Rose" says, "It's the soul afraid of dying that never learns to live."

Q: I have this deep-seated fear that no one likes me; thus, I spend a lot of my time doing things I don't really want to do in order to please others.

A: When you feel that others don't like you, it is a message to yourself that you don't like yourself. You attract to you as you think. If you don't like yourself, or are so intent on others liking or not liking you, then you will create that reflection of yourself in your environment. Learn to be good to yourself, to nourish yourself. Don't wait for a special occasion to wear perfume or dress up or to take a bubble bath. Do it now because you love yourself and want to be as good to yourself as you possibly can. As you come to love and appreciate yourself, the love within you can come forth and you will automatically draw to you those individuals who love you and love to be with you.

Q: I want to change my job, but I am afraid that I won't be able to find one that pays as well or that I will be happy doing.

A: Sit quietly and write out a list of those elements that you would like to have in a job. After you have put down everything that you can think of, take a moment to reflect on the list. Take a deep breath, close your eyes and imagine the white light, the creative force of the universe coming down through the top of your head and flowing through your body. After you have the white light flowing strongly yet calmly throughout your body, visualize the future job exactly as you would like to have it, being sure to put yourself in the picture. Put it in a pink balloon and let go of it, affirming that it or something better will come to you. There is nothing more you need to do.

Q: I often feel my intuition telling me to do something, but I am afraid to follow it. What if it's wrong?

A: You'll never know if it's right or wrong unless you act on it. Our real intuition is always right. We may have to work and practice in order to sort out our chattering mind from our inner wisdom, our real source of knowledge. The only way to sort this out is to act on our intuitive hunches, to follow the feeling, the energy, where it leads us. The more we ignore it, either the weaker it will become, the more confused our lives will be, or the louder it will yell, but by then usually a rock has dropped on our head.

Q: I find I am letting my fears get the best of me. I am afraid to go out of the house, afraid to drive my car, afraid to see others, in short, afraid to live.

A: When your fears get the best of you, as yours have, it is time to seek professional counseling. You need to work with someone who will help you see clearly how you are letting irrational fears control your life. There are professionals who are familiar with past-life regression, relaxation therapy, and the law of the universe. This is the type of individual that you need to seek out in order to regain control of your life. There's nothing wrong in asking for help when we need it.

Q: It seems that I am hearing you say that if we trusted the universe, the higher order of things, we would have no fears.

A: Fear is being out of touch with the master plan of the universe, the universal energy that flows through everyone. When we trust that it is there, guiding and protecting us, what more do we need?

Q: If there is this master plan, then why does it allow suffering and pain and the miseries of the world?

A: The miseries of the world that we see with our human eyes are merely a reflection of parts of our inner selves that need healing. They are also events that we have created in this lifetime to help us grow, and to fully experience life. After all, if there is no experience of loss or aloneness, how can we experience love; suffering, that we have joy; and pain, a signal from our body that something is wrong, that we are healthy.

MEDITATION

Enter your relaxed state, watching your breathing and letting the white light flow through your body. Feel the white light extend outward from your heart into the universe. Notice the warmth and energy that you feel when you do this. Ask your higher self to be with you and to protect you from any thought or feeling that is less than beneficial to you and your well-being. Continue to feel relaxed; ask to be shown what you are afraid of. When you hear or see something that you fear, look at it in great detail. What is the worst possible scenario? When you think that you have a clear picture of the "worst that could happen," imagine, in any way that you can, that you are giving it to your higher self to take care of. Trust that you have released it.

During the day, whenever you feel your logical self creating fear(s), tell yourself, "I can create these fears if I like, but I'm going to give them to my higher self to take care of."

Make a list of your fears. Beside each fear write down how it is keeping you from living fully.

If I Had My Life to Live Over
I'd like to make more mistakes next time.
I'd relax. I would limber up. I would be sillier
Than I have been this trip. I would take fewer
Things seriously. I would take more chances.
I would take more trips. I would climb more
Mountains and swim more rivers. I would eat
More ice cream and less beans. I would perhaps
Have more actual troubles. But I would have fewer
Imaginary ones.

You see, I'm one of those people who live
Sensibly and Sanely, Hour after Hour, Day
After Day. Oh, I've had my moments, and if
I had it to do over again, I'd have more of
Them. In fact, I'd try to have nothing else.
Just moments, one after another, instead of
Living so many years ahead of each day.
I've been one of those persons who never
Goes anywhere without a thermometer, a hot
Water bottle, a rain coat, and a parachute.
If I had to do it again, I would travel
Lighter than I have.

If I had my life to live over,
I would start barefoot earlier
In the spring and stay that way
Later in the fall. I would go to more dances,
I would ride more merry-go-rounds.
I would pick more daisies.

Nadine Satir,
85 years old,
Louisville, KY

Life must be lived as play, playing certain games, making sacrifices, singing and dancing, and then a man will be able to propitiate the gods.

Plato

INTUITI♥NS
Seeing With The Heart

Play
Chapter Eight

We are here to play. If we are in touch with our intuition and listening and following our heart, then our work is play. There is no separation of what we are doing from what we really desire to do.

Sometimes we lose sight of the fact that we need to have play in our lives when we become embroiled in the problems of life, which we have created for learning. In fact, there are times when we become so goal-oriented we forget what it is to be playful, to be free, to not be concerned with what others think of us.

It is only through play that we can relax. When we are under stress and uptight about the affairs of our work, we are unable to hear our inner wisdom and our heart.

Play is listening, feeling and experiencing. In order to awaken the child within us, we must be willing to play, to use our imagination, to be creative, to pretend. By being playful and by listening to our hearts, we are able to let go of old belief systems and open up to the various ways that our intuition speaks to us.

The Beginning:

You can't fool yourself. You know how you feel about your inner wisdom, your intuition. If you don't trust it, you will need to take small steps, one at a time, in order to rebuild your confidence its ability to bring valuable information to you.

Intuitive individuals are risk-takers, not motivated by inflexibility or a need for security, confident and independent. If your self-esteem is low, or if you trust others more than you trust yourself, then you are programming your intuition to fail you.

Notice the affirmations you give yourself on a daily basis. Do you say, "That problem is too difficult for me; I'll never find the answer?" Or, do you intuitively know that all answers are within you, and that if you ask a question, and let go of it, the answer will come?

"You have to ask a clear question and you ask one question at a time," Don Juan taught Carlos Castaneda. This is wise and important advice. You have to know what it is you want to get. Once you can ask the question the answer is before you. To ask more than one question at a time adds confusion to your answers, because you still get your answers, but they come all at once!

Exercises

#1

• Find a situation or a problem to which you would

like an answer.
- Write down on paper all of the things that you
  know about the situation.
- Write down what you would like to know
  about the situation.
- Follow the meditation exercise at the end of
  this chapter, which takes you to your guide in
  order to help you obtain the answers.
- Write down what you were told during the
  meditation, and see what additional questions
  come to mind.
- Let go of the situation and be patient.

#2

Several times during the day say to yourself,
"Tonight I will remember a dream that will bring me
information about ___ (this situation, problem, etc.).
Before retiring, relax and say to yourself, "I will
dream and I will remember the dream which will
give me information about ___."

#3

Write down all of the questions that you can think
of. Ask about your present life, future, relationships,
etc. Be aware of the answers that pop into your head
as soon as you formulate the questions.

#4

Take a walk. Guess who the next person that you
meet on the street will be. Male/female, old/young,
what they will have on, etc.

#5

Guess the amount of your next grocery bill without mentally trying to do the calculations in your
head. Guess the amount of gas your car will need
when you fill the tank.

#6

Pretend that you are someone else, an inner being that lives inside of you. Have a friend ask you questions about your life, future, health, someone else's life and future.

#7

Sit with a friend. Close your eyes and mentally ask to be in harmony with that individual. When you have been sitting for three minutes, take turns saying to each other the thoughts or images that have been coming to mind. Express how you feel, or if you have any physical discomfort.

#8

Center (relax) yourself. Go outside and find a tree. Mentally ask the tree questions from the four directions: From the north, ask the tree what it tells you; from the east, how does it feel being a tree?; from the south, how are you feeling?; and from the west, what do you sense?

#9

With two other individuals take turns choosing a season or time of day, and think about it. Give no physical signs of what you have picked. Ask others in the group what they have picked up. In the same way, pick an age and think about it.

#10

Sit and imagine that you are traveling to another city or to someone's home. What do you see? Explore the site in detail. Look for unusual objects or things taking place. Check out what you saw with the actual location.

#11

Imagine that someone whom you know is a rose. How does the rose look? Is it a new bud, barely open, or is it fully developed? Look at the stem and where the base of the rose is. Is it in water, a vase, the earth, or just in the air? What does this tell you about the person? Ask your mind for the answer. The first thing that comes to you is usually the correct answer.

We don't give our mind credit for knowing an answer or for being able to interpret the information it has given us. For example, you might ask a question about someone using the rose exercise in #11. Let us imagine that instead of seeing a red rose you saw a white rose that was fully open. Perhaps your first inclination is to say, "I don't know what that means." Ask your mind. It will immediately tell you something like white means age, enlightenment, health, etc., and that fully open implies an open individual. Trust what you get.

MEDITATION

Put yourself in your relaxed state and draw the white light in, down and through your body. Practice your deep breathing, watching your breath flow in and out of your body as the white light also moves through. After you have done this for a while, ask that you make contact with your highest source of information, your guide, counselor, or whatever else you may wish to call it. When the counselor appears, ask whatever questions you desire. Thank the counselor for the guidance you have received during this meditation.

EXERCISE 1:

Write down the last time you had an intuitive hunch and acted upon it.

Write down the last time you had an intuitive hunch and didn't act upon it. What happened?

How do you get your intuitive hunches?

EXERCISE 2A:
Relax. Take a deep breath. Imagine that you are surrounded by a warm white light. Think of the things you like about your life, relationships, job.

EXERCISE 2B:
Now focus on the present moment. Try to solve a particular problem you are facing in one of these areas. Look to see who is with you and what you are doing to remedy the situation.

EXERCISE 3A:
Write down three problems you would like to have the answers to.

1.

2.

3.

EXERCISE 3B:

Take a quiet moment to reflect on the problem. Using a pack of crayons, draw a picture that describes how you feel about one (or more) of the three problems you put on the preceding page.
What insight have you gained from the drawing? Look to see what colors you used, where you colored intensely, where you colored lightly, and where you didn't color at all.

EXERCISE 3C:

Ask a friend what they see in the picture. Don't tell them what the picture is about. Let them "intuit" the information.

EXERCISE 3D:

Draw the picture as you would like to have the situation resolved. Don't forget to put yourself in the picture and use the color pink to surround the entire image. Shakti Gawain says that pink is the color of the heart and to use it brings harmony to that which we are creating.

EXERCISE 4:

Pay attention to your "awareness." What are you aware of at this moment? Is this awareness something inside or a fantasy?

Direct your awareness to something you are not presently aware of. Is it inside or outside of yourself?

Direct your attention to the small toe on your left foot. What are you aware of now? Are you aware of the small toe on your right foot?

Let your awareness wander. See where it takes you. Focus your awareness on your body. What is tense? What is relaxed? How are you holding your shoulders? Your head? Your upper arms?

EXERCISE 5A:

The word "belief" comes from "be for me." You have an experience, and I accept your word or experience as true for me. Prior to the use of language we didn't have belief systems; we just *knew* things, because we personally experienced them. Through the ages we have come to believe in things which we have not experienced. It is important, as we learn to listen to our hearts, that we not accept beliefs without an experience to back them up. Belief systems without experience can become confusing and limit our own "knowingness."

Letting go of belief systems can be frightening. How do we balance what we have been taught in our institutions with what we are attempting to learn today? There is a balance and you must learn to trust it. Begin with looking at your present-day belief systems.

WHAT DO YOU BELIEVE IN?

On the left side of this page, write down ten things that you believe in. Now, beside each of these things, write down why you hold these beliefs:

Believe in	Why you believe
1._____	_____
2._____	_____
3._____	_____
4._____	_____
5._____	_____
6._____	_____
7._____	_____
8._____	_____
9._____	_____
10._____	_____

Are these valid beliefs?
Do they come from experience?

EXERCISE 5B:

Write down ten things you don't believe in. Beside each of these things, write down why you don't believe in these things.

Don't believe in	Why you don't believe
1._____	_____
2._____	_____
3._____	_____
4._____	_____
5._____	_____
6._____	_____
7._____	_____
8._____	_____
9._____	_____
10._____	_____

Are your reasons valid?

EXERCISE 6A:

Write down ten adjectives that describe yourself:

1._____

2._____

3._____

4._____

5._____

6._____

7._____

8._____

9._____

10._____

EXERCISE 6B:

With your non-dominant hand, write down ten adjectives that describe yourself:

1. _____   6. _____

2. _____   7. _____

3. _____   8. _____

4. _____   9. _____

5. _____   10._____

Now compare the lists. Is there a difference in the way you described yourself?

Each hand taps into a different part of your brain. The left side of your brain is more logical and analytical. The right side is more intuitive, creative, sensing, and feeling. If both lists were similar, then you are effectively working with communicating between the two hemispheres.

You must begin to trust yourself.
If you do not
then you will forever be looking to others
to prove your own merit to you,
and you will never be satisfied.

You will always be asking
others what to do,
and at the same time
resenting those from whom
you seek such aid.

Jane Roberts,
The Nature of Personal Reality

Trust
Chapter Nine

We have been conditioned by our society that what we can't see, touch, taste, or feel doesn't exist. Our educational system values analytical reasoning. Little support is given the artistic or creative child unless they attend a special school for the gifted and talented.

Our religious institutions have instilled the concept of a God who sits in the heavens with a long, grey beard and doles out rewards and punishments according to our acts in life. In western society, no value is given to the possibility that just maybe this isn't the only life we have led, that just maybe we aren't expected to get it (perfection) right in one single time around.

It is little wonder that after all of this conditioning

we find ourselves unable to trust that thought that pops into our head, or that feeling that seems to come out of the blue but brings with it good, valuable information.

Trusting your intuition automatically implies that you must take a risk. You must risk being wrong, or having your friends think you are foolish because you can't give a rational reason for what you are doing, and possibly losing friends because they can't stand to be with someone who does things, in their eyes, on a whim. You must risk change in yourself, in relationships, in your environment. You must risk that you will find more to life than you ever thought existed, that you do have answers—answers that work and are meaningful. You must risk your security in order to know that the inner voice guides and directs you in every facet of your life and while you may not always be able to see where you are going, you trust your intuition and know that you are in the right place at the right time.

Begin to get in touch with your inner voice by learning how you receive your answers. As was stated in Chapter One, there are many different ways that intuitive information is received. Do you have a thought suddenly pop into your head? Are you able to check the thought out to see if the information is valid? Feedback is very important in learning to trust ourselves. If your intuition says take a warm coat even though the thermometer is reading 80 degrees, do you take the coat or do you rationalize just why you couldn't possibly need a coat in weather like this? When a freak snowstorm hits, you have verification that your inner voice was accurate.

Remember that intuition speaks softly and is very patient. You may hear, and ignore, the same message again and again. It doesn't make demands or try to make you feel guilty. You may be hearing the message while you are driving home from work or out running. It doesn't necessarily come when you sit down and meditate; you may not be relaxed in this state, or you may be trying too hard to receive your answer.

Learn to act on your physical feelings, that barometer that was discussed earlier in this book. When you start to listen to your physical body and follow what it tells you, you begin to get in the flow of knowing the answers and the questions.

Ask for help from the universe. Many individuals feel that they can only ask for help in matters of a highly spiritual nature. You are in this physical body for a reason. Your inner voice is a part of your physical body and is as interested in whether or not you are following a diet that is healthy to you as in whether you can meditate for forty minutes and see your guardians and the white light.

Look for external signs of verification as well as internal ones (remember Boston?). Sometimes, if we have been ignoring our inner wisdom, we may find a friend saying something to us that we have been hearing, but ignoring, for months. Or someone may give you a book that just happens to have the answer you have been looking for. There are many ways to receive information if we are open to them.

Some examples of your intuition vs. your rational, analytical self:

Intuition: I would like to separate from my business partner and go out on my own. Something doesn't feel right here.

Rational: I'll never succeed on my own. I'll be financially strapped, I'll lose his friendship.

Intuition: Although I know the party tonight will be talked about for weeks, I would rather stay home and read a book.

Rational:	People will think I'm not being social. The hostess will think I don't like him/her. I should go; it's the proper thing to do.
Intuition:	Call Robert.
Rational:	Robert will think I'm chasing him, trying to trap him, pestering him. (It may actually be fact that Robert wants to talk to you but hasn't been able to reach you.)

You get the idea. One can always think of rational reasons why they shouldn't do what their intuition tells them to do. Often the most commonly used rational excuse is that "it isn't logical." Logic does not always go hand in hand with your intuitive voice.

Q: There are times when I follow my intuition and it turns out to be wrong. How can I tell when it is right and when it is wrong?

A: Your intuition is always right, but there are times when we misinterpret what we see or sense. We may think that we "see" a beautiful swimming pool when, in fact, we see a sewage treatment facility. As you learn how your mind brings information to you, you will be able to use your mental pictures or sounds along with your physical feelings. The combination will help you interpret your information accurately. Always know that you can ask your dreams to bring you the answer, because it is not as easy to control and manipulate our dreams.

Q: It is easy for me to trust what a psychic tells me, but when it comes to my own inner wisdom I fall short. How can I change this?

A: When you consistently give your power away to someone who you think has all of the answers, especially for yourself, you are giving your intuition the message that you don't trust it. Begin to "listen" to your intuition on a daily basis and follow the advice it gives. With each act of faith your own intuitive process will become stronger. Only when you feel you need someone to reflect back to you what you are creating, or when you feel that your emotions are clouding your answers, should you seek answers from a source outside of yourself. Even then, see how the answers that you are given resonate with your inner being.

Q: When I get answers from inside, I think that I am just making it up. How do I know when I'm not, that it's not just my imagination?

A: You are making it up, but your imagination is real. You can call it guessing if you like . . . but you want to learn to "guess" with a ninety-five percent accuracy rate. Don't worry about whether or not you are making it up; we make everything up, including our entire lives!

MEDITATION

Sit quietly in a place where you feel very comfortable. Close your eyes and watch or listen to the thoughts that travel through your mind. Pay attention, but do not hold on to any one particular thought; just let it pass by as a cloud would drift across the sky. Notice your inner feelings about these thoughts . Do you feel anxious? comfortable? neutral? Move your awareness to your heart and see how it feels right now. Imagine that your heart is radiating white light out from you and into the universe. Repeat the following affirmation to your heart and to the universe,

"I know that there is more to life than what can be seen. I want to get in touch with this knowledge and to learn to trust it. I am willing to travel where I cannot see and know what I cannot know. I am willing to listen to the voice that has no sound and to the message of my heart. I trust."

Continue to sit quietly and ask yourself these

questions: What is keeping me from trusting my intuition at this point in my life?

What previously kept me from trusting my intuition?

What do I need to do right now to increase my trust in myself?

To whom do I give away my "power?" (Whom do you trust with answers more than you trust yourself?)

When was the last time I heard an intuitive message and acted on it?

When was the last time I heard an intuitive message and didn't act on it?

Tell yourself that you will remember these answers and use them to help you further your own intuitive awareness and trust of yourself. Thank your "heart" for its help in this meditation.

EXERCISE

The next time you feel you have an intuitive hunch about something . . . *act* on it. See what happens. If it was from your heart it will prove to be good, valuable information. If it was off the mark, e.g., your ego talking, the information may prove less than accurate or complete. Remember how you felt when you got the information; did you take it to your heart and see how it felt there?

*The moment one definitely commits oneself,
then providence moves too.
All sorts of things occur to help one that
would never otherwise have occurred.
A whole stream of events issues from the
decisions, raising in one's favor all manner of
unforeseen incidents and meetings and
material assistance which no man could have
dreamed would have come his way.
Whatever you can do or dream you can,
begin it. Boldness has genius, power and
magic in it. Begin it now.*

Goethe

Visualization
Chapter Ten

Someone takes a step, commits oneself, and things begin to happen. Is it because we are able to "read" our future? Or does it happen because we create it? And does it make any difference?

Many books and articles have been written about the power of the mind and of visualization. Still, until it becomes a reality for us, many fail to believe it. It is simply too good to be true. It's magic! But magic with substance. Which brings to surface the question, if we can have anything we desire, why is there poverty, suffering, etc.? In short, why don't we always get what we want? Or do we?

Let's examine the questions. If we don't get what we want, perhaps it is because we are unclear on exactly what we want, or that we are willing to settle for less. We may begin by saying we want "X" but will settle for "Y" and will actually accept "Z." This confuses the universe, which has an order. What our thoughts are could be viewed as a photograph slightly out of focus. If you ask for stew, that's exactly what you are going to get—stew! Only when you have a clear picture and a clear goal will you achieve your heart's desires.

The magic behind this theory is that everything that you have in your life now was at some point in the past, just a thought. You may not have been aware of it then, but it was a thought. Even today was a thought before it actually became a reality. Consider, if you placed too much emphasis or worried about some particular event, then in all probability it took place, just as you thought it would—for better or worse. If today was muddled, then your expectations of it were muddled.

Our thoughts became our reality and our reality seems to be common sense after we have lived it.

In order to pattern, creatively visualize, or manifest things in your life, you must be willing to accept that what you think, you are. Whatever you can do or dream, you can do. So begin it.

A former state trooper for the state of New York is so adept at manifesting that he is, at times, afraid to think. He knows his thoughts will manifest. One morning I, too, became aware of the power of manifesting when I decided to manifest a rose. At 4:15 p.m. that day a friend called from another city, telling me about a great song he had just heard, "The Rose," which was my favorite song.

The next day I decided that I hadn't named the rose; so I would again see what I could manifest in the form of a rose. As I was driving down main street I looked up at the theater marquee and there it was—a movie by the title, "The Name of the Rose."

This continued for one more day, until I manifested a picture of an American Beauty rose from a friend's garden. A week later, I was having dinner with a friend in New England, and in the center of the table were three real roses, one for each of the roses I had manifested.

My move to Providence, RI, was another lesson in manifestation. I decided that I shouldn't have to look for an apartment, that I would manifest it. The day I began, I only had two hours to look and there were only three apartments in the newspaper which interested me. Of the three, there were only two I had time to see. I knew the first wasn't what I wanted, and I thought the second was too expensive.

However, when I went to see the second apartment, the landlord was in the process of renovating it, and it met all my criteria and more—white walls, fireplace, newly refinished floors, two bedrooms (it turned out to have three; I had overlooked one), easy access to move in my grand piano, and I could have pets. Additionally, it was in a wonderful location— close to some friends, a plus I didn't think I was patterning for. If I had mentally tried to picture all the "pluses," I probably would not have added location, feeling I was being too selfish.

EXERCISE

How can you manifest what you want? By following the simple guidelines below, you may even surprise yourself with the results.

- Have clear intent. Know what you want. And know that you have to devote some time to the thought in order to get what you want. Then release it. Know that the universe will bring it to you.

- Byron Gentry, a healer from Oklahoma, uses clapping to help manifest health, etc. (I use a combination of things I learned from Byron, from Shakti Gawain, and from my own source of wisdom.) Have a clear picture of what it is you want to manifest. Clap once to put your head in a positive polarity and your feet in a negative polarity. Clap three times to dissolve any emotional energy around the situation; then clap five times to increase the *velocity* of universal energy coming into your body. Finally, clap five times to increase the *amount* of universal energy coming into your body.

- Picture or feel the situation as you would like it to be. Put yourself in the picture. Put this picture in a pink balloon, take it to your favorite spot and release it and as you say: "This, or something better, now manifests for me in perfectly satisfying and harmonious ways for the highest good of all concerned."

Note: It is important to release what it is that you want. It has to reach the energy of the universe in order for it to come back to you.

The exercises above are to help focus awareness. Think of what you want and it will appear if you will invest the time and follow the ritual. IT DOES WORK!

When you get into it, there may be instances when you will wonder if you are actually creating your life, or fantastically in tune with what the universe is sending your way. When you are in harmony with the universe you will realize it doesn't make any difference. Things will work out exactly as they are supposed to, and on schedule.

The simplest way to manifest those things spiritual is to ask—ask the universe, your highest source of information, to help you. Ask it to help you get information from your dreams, to experience or to be aware of an out-of-body state, to know what it is you are supposed to be doing. Remember, as you are asking, you have to continue to put forth some energy on your own behalf in order to move towards your goal.

I may ask for a number of interesting bookings with my workshops. But I have to write the letters, make the calls, and do the organizational things necessary for the workshops to be created. In the end, the workshops I actually book may not come from any of the contacts I made originally. But the bookings do come, and I always find I am in the right place at the right time.

Trust that the universe knows what it is doing. It does.

INTUITIONS
Seeing With The Heart

The Game
Chapter Eleven

In the end it all boils down to the fact that life is just a game, a magnificent game that we are playing. As we play the game we invent the rules, and one of the rules is the fact that it is never too late to change the road we are traveling. Intuition helps us know/ create the rules and change the rules or the road.

Rule one: You chose to be here; so be here now. Living in the moment is everything. All too often we're living in the past, or the future, but not the now. Do you know what it's like to take a walk and enjoy where you are at that point in time, without letting your mind race ahead to what you have to do when you return? It's difficult for us, as human beings, to keep our thoughts only on the present. We have been programmed to look backward or forward in time. Only when we are in the present can we create the future; sounds paradoxical, but it's true.

Being here now means enjoying exactly where you are at any given time. Don't be anxious for tomorrow; it will be here soon enough. Then you will be looking ahead to next week or next month or next year. To-morrow will take care of itself, but today you can be here and feel the heart-felt messages that come to you in the now. Look at it this way . . . what if there is no tomorrow? What if the only thing you can be sure of is today? What then? Would you do things differ-ently? Would you be angry at someone you love? Would you be so obsessive about whether or not the breakfast dishes were washed or the lawn mowed? Would you refrain from telling someone that you love them?

Rule two: Because you chose to be here, you also chose your body, your parents, your friends and your present life situation. No one has done anything to you, but you. There may be times when you are un-able to see what you were supposed to get out of a given situation, but you can rest assured that when you are in your total state of knowing you set up the situation and lessons you wanted to learn this time around.

Rule three: You get what you want. The law of the universe—our own ability to create and manifest—gives us our hearts' desires. When you sincerely put out a clear request, it will come to you.

Rule four: Whatever you think of strongly, or put your energies into, you attract into your life. If you are negative in your attitude, then you will attract people and circumstances in your life to reinforce that belief system. If, on the other hand, you are a positive, opti-mistic person, your life will reflect back to you one of divine order, happiness, and well-being.

Rule five: It is an abundant universe. Too often we think of the universe as being "limited" in food, wealth, natural resources, etc. The only limits in the universe are those which we impose on ourselves and our reality.

Rule six: You will have magnificant bursts of spiritual growth, to be followed by what seems to be a period of quiet. It is during these times of quiet that the most is happening; this is when your unconscious is being its most creative. Part of our learning in this lifetime is to learn patience. This means not forcing the rose, but letting it unfold in its own time.

Rule seven: "You cannot discover new oceans until you have the courage to lose sight of the shore." (Author unknown)

Rule eight: Realize that you are asleep, trying to wake up. In so doing you will begin to unravel the mysteries of life and open your heart.

Rule nine: The only thing you know is what you don't know. In fact, you don't know what you don't know!

Rule ten: "To everything there is a season, and a time to every purpose under the heaven."
—Ecclesiastes 3:1

Rule eleven: "Ask, and it shall be given you; seek, and ye shall find; knock, and it shall be opened unto you."
—Matthew 7:7

Post Script

After publishing *Intuitions,* most of the mail I received contained questions about relationship. Now that I am in a full-time, committed relationship, I find that many of the questions I wrote about in the First Edition haven't gone away; they are still there; they are just different.

It was originally my intention to write a sequel to *Intuitions,* but I couldn't decide exactly what I wanted to write. I knew that I wanted to bring some closure to my search for my relationship with self, as well as my search for my "twin soul." I started several "books," only to leave them on the computer while I "thought about" writing. I discovered other interesting things about myself, such as the fact that I am close to being a "wanna-be" writer. I talk about writing a lot, but I don't sit down and write, just as I don't sit down and practice the piano. Then, I read about a famous writer who stood in front of a seminar and said, "How many of you want to be writers?" All of the hands went up. And the famous writer said, "Then go home and write," and sat down.

There are many individuals who have better stories, more correct grammar, more exciting experiences to tell, but they don't write; they don't put it down. I began to realize that this *is* life, that I wasn't getting anything done while waiting for inspiration, and after much procrastination I decided to publish this updated, second edition.

At the close of *Intuitions,* I had left my husband, job, and home in Virginia and headed for Providence, RI. I was going strictly on trust in the universe, because I didn't have a steady income, and I had signed a lease on an apartment in Providence (for more than I was making in my newly formed training and consulting business). In fact, almost all of my business contacts were in Virginia!

Still, everything seemed to be falling into place. The apartment I found was in the process of being renovated (it was gutted when I saw it), and the landlady kindly agreed to let me select the paint colors. She allowed pets (I had two dogs), and there was easy access to the first floor so that I could move in my grand piano. I had unconsciously managed to create everything that I wanted, even an extra bedroom that I didn't know about until the day I moved in. This extra space later turned out to be significant.

The year that I spent in Providence was a year of processing my inner self, as I constantly asked myself if I had made the "right" decision to leave. As in the past, my dreams gave me my answers. I asked, "What's going on in my life?" (I would tell you to be more specific and less general with your questions.) I dreamed that there was an airplane waiting to take off on the runway. Before I would board I said, "I have to go to my exercise studio." When I got to the studio there was a "Closed" sign across the door. I returned to the airport, walked by Katherine Ross (star of *The Graduate)* and boarded the plane. Now, I find it interesting that not only did I graduate from that life, I married a Robinson, lived in Scarborough, and, of course, had an herb garden. Was my intuition telling me all of that in just one dream, or was I creating my future in the dream and does it make any difference? At the least, the dream told me that there was nothing I could work out. It was time to go.

The next significant dream I had in resolving my feelings about leaving Virginia and my husband came when I was doing my security bit; "If I had stayed in Virginia I would have this beautiful home and lots of security. No romance, but lots of security." I had a dream in which my husband and I were driving down a street that turned out to be a dead end. We got out and walked past numerous dead bodies toward our home. I found myself asking the question about staying in our new home. I walked into a house that had no back wall, tilted on its foundation and, once I was inside, the floors became squishy and covered with plastic. I looked out the window and saw that the house was sinking into the mud. I turned to leave, and as I was leaving, I noticed that I was carrying a bag of trash in my hand. "I don't need this," I thought. I dropped the trash, crawled over some broken stones and left.

I had one more dream in which my husband and I shook hands. At this point I knew that this phase of my life was complete and I was ready to move forward. Within a week Michael walked into my life.

Michael

In the first edition of *Intuitions* , I wrote about soul mates and twin souls. Now, five years later, I am not as sure about these concepts as I was then. I have no doubt that there are very special souls with whom we connect, but as with the dolphins, putting our words and concepts on these energies may limit them. Never in my wildest imagination could I have known what Michael would be like!

When I left Virginia, I knew that I was not with the man with whom I would do my life's major work. I didn't know who he would be, but I thought that he might be a physician, because I was working in the medical field and this seemed logical to me. Of course, logic has nothing to do with the Universe and its order (and humor).

Three days after I left Virginia, I substituted for another trainer at the Monroe Institute. I was a basket case that week. The most I could do was coordinate the technical aspects of the program while my co-trainer handled all of the emotional crises. It was mid-week when I realized that there was one participant I didn't know at all. This is highly unusual, because I was in a seven-day residential setting with only 1~20 participants. That evening I found myself (accidentally?) sitting next to him at dinner.

"I find it very intimidating that you can read my mind," he said.

"I know, why is that?" and why, I wondered, do I have this intense feeling in my heart when he asks that question? Do I intimidate all men? Does this mean I'll never find my partner?

Before he could respond to my answer, my co-trainer pulled me away from the table.

The last day, as we were preparing to depart, I felt a tap on my shoulder. It was the same man. "I understand that you do readings. I don't know what they are, but would you do one for me? I would like you to help me figure out a dream I had the other night."

After he described the dream, there were two things I was sure of. First, this was a man who was truly in touch with the oneness of the universe when he skied, or participated in sports; secondly, the woman in his dream was a very special soulmate who had showed up at this point in time.

"What can you tell me about my soulmate in this life?"

"You've touched her hand. I also see the letter M. (I later pondered if the M was for me? Or was I just wrong on this account?)

"It's Winter," Michael thought but didn't say anything. He did start to think of every woman whose hand he had touched. He later said that whenever he thought about what I had said, he would think that it was me.

"No, it's not her. She's the teacher!" Then, once more, he would try to think of all of the women whose hand he had touched.

During the following summer, I was writing *Intuitions*, and deadlines seemed to be the only thing on my mind. I was also paying strict attention to my dream life in order to process and to research how dreams worked for me. One of my discoveries in living alone in a new apartment was that my two dogs loved to get up early and go out early (5:00 a.m.). I got into the habit of letting them out and going back to bed. It was during these early morning hours of sleep that I would dream the answers to my dream questions, have lucid dreams or out-of-body experiences, or have any other dream state I was writing about.

This particular morning I was in an out-of-body state with a friend of mine who was a physician. We were trying to pull one of his friends out of her body, and we were engrossed in the process. Suddenly a "stranger" appeared, kissed me and (I thought) hypnotized me.

"How dare you come into my dream and kiss me!" I remember saying, as I felt a green ocean roll over me. I later noticed that in my dream journal I had written that I liked the kiss of this tall, blonde man whom I identified as an *alien.*

Later that summer, I had numerous dreams about preparing for marriage as well as dreams of closure with my ex-husband, John.

I not only write down dreams, I write down words and sentences that I hear in the night. On December 22, 1987, I wrote down several "shorts": exhibits, eating, talking with others, looking at muscles, **waiting for Michael.**

Immediately prior to this dream, I had been studying anatomy in a class in which we sculpted the body out of clay. As I created my clay body, I decided that it would be a man. I thought, "If we manifest our thoughts, why don't I put my thoughts about what I

139

want into this clay model? I'll make me a man!"

What I was realizing as I did this was that his looks didn't matter. I couldn't even list all of the things that I wanted in my partner, other than that he be romantic, sensitive and spiritual, (by my definitions) and that he would hold my hand. On the other hand, I had a good idea of what I did not want in a relationship.

There were many other things that I can look back upon and see how I was nesting, preparing for a significant relationship. I purchased all new linens, dishes and gowns that I did not wear but let hang in the closet in anticipation.

Early in December, while I was conducting a workshop in Boston, one of the participants (Stan) came up to me at a break. "I'm attending your workshop because my roommate said that it would be great!"

"That's nice. Who is your roommate?"

"Michael Robinson."

"I don't know a Michael Robinson."

Stan shifted his weight and looked as if he were mentally computing my response. "Yes, you met him at the Monroe Institute last spring. He lives in Maine."

These are the situations I hate to get myself into, because here is someone who clearly knows who I am—so much so he sends his roommate to my workshop. I should know who he is; after all, I spent seven days in an intensive program with him! I subtly try to bring up a picture of Michael Robinson in my mind, something that should be quite easy for me to do. No such luck. No picture. I would have to take this man's word for it that I know a Michael Robinson.

I did remember meeting someone from Maine. In fact, any time I thought of Maine, I thought of how nice it would be to visit that state, and each time I made plans to do so they fell through. As a child, I was fascinated by the State of Maine; I thought it was the state that looked like a mitten. And, didn't all of the mystery writers live there?

A few weeks after the workshop, I received a call from Stan setting up a reading with me for Michael. "Just drop him a card and tell him when and where to show up."

"This must be some unusual man," I thought. "What does he do that I can send him a card and he will be free enough to drop whatever he is doing and come see me?"

Our reading was scheduled for January 14, 1988 at 5:00 p.m. in Boston. (I later learned that Michael had driven to Boston a week earlier thinking that the appointment was that week.) When he walked in the door, I remembered him. "He's very cute," I thought to myself as I said, "That is a gorgeous ski jacket!"

No, I didn't realize that this man was someone with whom I was spending eternity. I did love his energy and found I talked about it a lot during the session and afterward. As Michael prepared to leave, he invited me to visit him and Stan in Maine that weekend. (I was planning a trip to L.L. Bean with a girlfriend.)

We did. And, they invited us to return in three weeks to go skiing with them. We did.

Stretching

I discovered a lot about myself that long weekend on the ski slopes. I am quick to tell others, "You can heal yourself. Look at your fears." Then I put on skis, look down the hill, and I find myself scared to death!

"I might hurt myself," I hear myself thinking.

"So what if you do? Can't you heal yourself?" My inner guidance is at work in full force.

Can I walk my talk? Can I learn to manipulate these sticks on my feet and stop them? I was certainly going to try.

The physical body is a wonderful mechanism for teaching us, not only when we are ill, but especially when we are healthy.

At the condo that weekend I got up in the morning and took my dogs out. (Yes, he let me bring my dogs and I was duly impressed.) I came back in, *sans* make-up and all of the stuff I thought I needed to make myself presentable, and smelled baked bread and freshly brewed coffee. What a marvelous experience. I was not accustomed to having a man in the kitchen creating such divine treats. The energy those four days was wonderful, not consciously sexual energy at all, but an energy that flowed just like the energy of being with the dolphins. It is wonderful, and sometimes it is the most noticeable when you step out of it.

Messages

It was two weeks later when I found myself in Arizona with my good friend Swami. We were spending time in Boynton Canyon in Sedona, when two ravens landed about four feet in front of me. From the corner of my eye, I saw Swami looking at me with one of her fantastic, knowing, smiles.

"Partnership is at hand," she said.

Later that evening, as we sat around a table in the small cabin we had rented, Swami pulled out her Mother Peace Tarot deck. "I have a layout that works for relationship. I have been using it for several weeks and it works every time."

"There is no one in my life right now, Swami. Read my lips—no one I can do a layout with." How, I wonder, do you tactfully tell a Swami to "bug off?"

"Come on, Winter. It's just for fun, and it works. Use anybody."

Finally, after what seemed an hour of saying,

"No," I gave in, "Oh, all right, use Michael."

"Who's Michael?"

"He's just a friend. That's all, just a friend. He's someone I was skiing with recently."

Swami began the layout. How I wish I had, at the least, written it down.

"He doesn't know what to do. This is a major, major transformational relationship."

To be honest, I don't think I was listening to all she was saying. I noticed her hand shaking and, for once and possibly the first time in her life, Swami seemed to have difficulty speaking.

"You're going to marry this man."

"Oh, Swami. Not Michael; he's just a friend. We both know I'm probably very close to another relationship, and I think that you are probably picking up on that energy." I finally convinced her I was right.

The last two days I was in Arizona, I was sick with a very strange flu. I felt as though something were trying to overtake me. All I could do was lie in bed and dream. The day I was to leave, I found myself having a lucid dream. By now I had learned that when I am lucid I can control my dreams and go into an out-of-body state.

"I want to be with my twin soul." Immediately I found myself making love with a man—a man with a marvelous energy. It didn't last long, because a girl-friend who was with me woke me up. I wasn't happy to have this wonderful dream experience end in this manner.

"Why did you do that?"

"I thought you were having a nightmare."

"Hardly." I remembered that she had made a crowing sound and scared the two ravens away when we were in Boynton canyon. "I wonder just what is going on here?"

At the time I was unaware that I had filled my

entire life with work and with this friend. There was no space for a man to be in my life, even though I said I wanted a relationship. Well, that's not quite true. Probably what helped me in the unconscious arena was the fact that I had a room in my apartment that was virtually empty. It was as though this room were waiting for him.

That day my friend left for the Middle East for work, and I returned to Rhode Island and placed a call to Michael. As I made the call, I remember thinking, "I hope his roommate doesn't answer. I really want to talk to Michael and yet I have no good excuse." (That was old stuff. Why do we need an excuse to talk to someone other than the fact that we want to?)

He answered.

I started the conversation with something like, "I called because I've been thinking about you. I was wondering if you had been thinking of me and if there was some type of telepathy going on."

"As a matter of fact, I have been. I've been in South Carolina on business, and during my travels I've been trying to read Carlos Castaneda. I kept thinking that I would like to talk with you about his writing."

"When do you have time? I'm free this weekend."

"I'm also free. I'll come down on Saturday morning. How long will it take me?"

This was amazing. Both of us were free. This was the first free weekend I had in a year. I told him it would take four hours to drive from Portland, ME, to Providence, RI.

I had my first date since my separation the night before Michael appeared on my doorstep. That was an eventful evening in many respects, because I found myself standing in the middle of my apartment and realizing that I was very happy. My career was going well; my book was selling; I was content.

"Where would a man fit into my life?" I was realizing that I didn't need a man to make me happy or fulfilled. I was happy and I felt fulfilled as a human and as a woman. (This is when, I think, the Universe intervenes, "Ah, ha! Now, you are ready. Try this!")

It would seem that Guidance gives us many practical jokes, tests, and lessons in discernment. My test that evening proved to be a date with a man very similar to my ex and his family. He was a banker/lawyer, very conservative, not into other realities at all and, to be honest, I am sure he thought I was quite wacky. I didn't play dating politics at all . . . I was quite above board about what I believe and what my career entailed. It is clear to me now that I needed this encounter as a reminder not to turn back. This type of relationship was not what I wanted, but because I had been in a similar setting for so long, it was what I was drawing to me.

It took Michael two hours to drive from Maine to Providence.

I was barely out of bed when he arrived. So I quickly attached leashes to Signe and Gisela, my dogs, handed the leashes to him, watched while they wrapped themselves around his long legs, and sent the three of them out the door while I woke up.

Castaneda

The day we were to talk of Castaneda, we went to Newport and walked the cliffs, looked at boats, and talked of magic and other unknowns of the Universe. At one point we walked out onto a rocky shoreline to see the waves and ocean more clearly, and I took his arm. I thought about what I was doing as I reached up to take hold of him, but it seemed like the prudent thing to do if I was to be able to maintain any semblance of agility on the slippery rocks.

As this long, fun-filled day came to a close, we

finally settled in to serious talk on the sofa (and no, it wasn't about us or romance). As I reflect back on that evening, I remember that it was chilly in the living room. So I pulled out an old Hudson's Bay blanket and threw it over the two of us as we sat and chatted. It seemed like a perfectly normal thing to do at the time. As we were talking (he was so close to me I could see the almost invisible, feathery tips of his eyelashes and the thin lines under his eyes that crinkled when he smiled), I realized that I was looking at him through something sheer, slightly transparent. I will call it a veil for lack of other words. The veil slowly began to lift and I recognized Michael for the first time.

One of my inner selves, most likely the "I am a proper, Southern woman," became loud and clear, "What do I do with this? Here I am with this cute, very eligible bachelor who probably has numerous women chasing after him. Do I tell him about this veil, about the dreams and out-of-body experiences I have had with him? What is he thinking right now? What can I say? And, worse yet, what am I going to do with this knowledge? How did I get myself into this?"

The reality of the situation was that I threw the blanket off, stood up and headed toward the bathroom. "I'm going to brush my teeth and go to bed." When all else fails, escape is always a good route to take. If there is one thing I can say for myself it is that I have always been a good runner, as a child and as an adult. This seemed like an opportune time to retreat.

I heard the front door open as Michael went out to the car to bring in his blue sleeping bag. Once inside, he tossed it on the futon in the guest room, turned and smiled at me. (By now, I was out of the bathroom, because one can only brush one's teeth for so long.) And then, did I step forward? Did he? I really don't know. All I remember is that Michael put his arms around me, gently kissed me good night and asked, "What are you thinking?"

"What are you thinking?"

"I asked you first."

Here was an excellent opportunity for me to walk my talk. Could I be honest and still maintain a friendship with this person I was coming to like so much? Could I tell only a partial truth and live with myself? What did I have to lose? Lots. If I were honest and it scared him, I would blow a wonderful friendship with someone with whom I was very comfortable. On the other hand, if I didn't tell the complete truth, we might remain as friends when there was potential for so much more. Was what I was feeling real? Was it just sexual energy?

I told him that I didn't want him to spend the night in the guest room.

So, there you have it. Some things are best left to the imagination. I will say that when Michael took me in his arms, I fit. I fit like I have never fit in anyone else's arms; it was as though we were made from a single mold, the two halves linking so perfectly.

After that night, I knew and I had no doubts about our relationship, but Michael, on the other hand, said he was trying to figure out just what was going on.

Two months later I moved in with Michael . . . two dogs, grand piano and all. This major move was finalized after an eventful car trip in which he expressed his reservations about our relationship, "If this relationship works."

"What do you mean if? Of course it's working!"

Michael was going back to past relationship failures in his life and reliving them. Other relationships had not worked out; thus, he was protecting his heart by putting forth the possibility that this one might not make it.

Commitment

On June 30,1988, we became engaged. That, also, was magical but in a different kind of way, a way that showed the humor in life. We wanted a special ring that would signify our commitment to each other. It was only a matter of minutes until I knew that my friend Joe, my running partner from Virginia and maker of fine jewelry, was the person to help us.

Michael called Joe, expressing to him what we had in mind. After making several telephone calls, Joe called back and said that his supplier had only one diamond which had the features that we were looking for. I could tell from Michael's expression that he was expecting news of a different sort.

"Only one? I wanted several to choose from."

I knew that if there were only one then it was the one for us. There would be no need to try to select from several. The one had made itself known. The day we went to select a setting and to look at the diamond was an exercise in laughter, and in letting go of ideas about material goods. Joe began to show us what a beautiful diamond this was as he pulled out another with which to compare it.

"You can always tell the difference by weighing the two." Then he proceeded to blow on the scale and show that the weight would change with a puff of wind!

In the course of the afternoon, he proceeded to drop the diamond and then, in all honesty, to lose it. It was after we lost it that we began to laugh at ourselves. This had to be our stone, there was such humor in the selection. The losing of the stone reminded us not to put so much significance into material goods. It is our commitment to each other, not the symbol that we use as commitment, that is important!

Joe found the diamond.

Messages

In hindsight I can see that I received many messages about my future partner. I can also see that I was very selective and edited the information which I took in. For instance, I had several dreams in which I was with a stranger who was tall and blonde. Because this description did not "fit" what I expected my twin soul to look like, I ignored these dreams. Perhaps, as Michael Talbot *(Holographic Universe)* would have said, there are several holograms which tell us of our future. I chose the one with the strongest energy, and the one I had been creating with Michael prior to reincarnating. Perhaps . . .

In looking back over my journals, I came across a tarot reading that a friend had done for me in November of 1987. "I see the beginning of romance. This man will be blonde, will live in the country, loves nature and home. He is well liked, honorable and sound in judgment."

Why did I ignore this? Because I had strong, physical feelings for a man I had met who was a physician and had dark hair and lived in Boston . . . downtown Boston.

I believe that the dark-haired man played a significant role in my life, part of which was to help me feel what it is like to be alive, to actually feel something! I didn't know I had such intense feelings until I met him. If ever I believed in a past life, or a simultaneous existence, it was when we were together, but I scared him. This was obvious and I refused to see it, as well as the fact that he also had many characteristics similar to my ex-husband. I now realize that Michael also has characteristics similar to both of these men, and this is neither good nor bad, it just is.

Having specific information about your future mate can be a hindrance if you aren't careful. If I had listened to the information that my partner would have blonde hair, I might have passed up many learning opportunities with brunettes, or I might have thought he was some other man with blonde hair. From time to time, Michael will say maybe it is still another man with blonde hair. Could be, but in my heart I think not.

I try not to give detailed information to others in instances such as this, but sometimes I slip and do so. I am sure there are some who would say I am avoiding the issues when I don't answer this type of question; however, I don't think my role is to tell anyone what to do about any relationship, because that would be giving me too much power.

Usually, I don't try to see someone's appearance, because of the reasons I mentioned above. In the long run, it doesn't make any difference. We won't hear or see information of this type until we are ready, and then the event is so close we will know it soon anyway. Psychic readings are the most fun when we look back into the past at what we knew, or what we were told. Then we have the Ah ha!

Ninety-nine percent of the letters I received after writing *Intuitions* were about relationships. Many of those writing either thought that they had found their twin soul, were very unhappy in their present relationship, or both.

I can't think of any time when I would advise an individual to leave a relationship for someone else. It is important to look at, and know, who you are and what you want before leaping into a relationship with another individual. If you aren't happy with yourself no one else will be able to make you happy and you will find yourself on the fast road to disaster. Not only that, you will recreate the same relationship again and again, because it is you doing the creating.

Listen to your inner voice speak to you about how you feel. Are you happy with your life? It is not your present partner who makes you miserable; only you can claim responsibility for how you feel. If you aren't happy, why aren't you happy? What are the things that you used to like to do that you no longer have time for? What is keeping you from doing them? Are these things fulfilling, or are they part of an endless search? Are they a way of keeping busy? Remember, we all change constantly. We are not the same person we were in the grocery store this morning, let alone the same person we were last year.

I did not leave my ex-husband for anyone other than myself. I wasn't happy. I didn't have the energy that I knew was once inside me. John didn't take the energy from me. I did. I allowed myself to assume a role that wasn't true to my spirit, and it eventually caught up with me. Perhaps I could have remained in my first marriage and worked things out; I don't know. The fact is I was changing, returning to my true self. I was not being and could not be the same person my husband married. To live, I felt that I had to leave.

In the fall of 1987, prior to meeting Michael, I was very busy with my career. In fact, I was in an airplane most of the time coming and going to various workshops and lectures. I am certain that part of this frantic pace had to do with the fear of failure, of starving, of becoming a "bag lady."

One day, I had arrived home from Dayton, OH, at 11:30 p.m. and I was departing on a 7:00 a.m. flight to Richmond, VA. I thought, "This is crazy. Here I am flying all over the country teaching others how to take control of their lives and I don't have control of my own. I don't have any private life and this I don't like."

I decided then and there I was going to have a private life come January, without giving up any income. (This was important. Frequently, if we are not clear about what we want to create, it comes out fuzzy or less than.) We say that we want X, but we'll take Y, and we'll settle for Z! How does the Universe know what to give us in these circumstances? If I had not made the statement about income, I might have found myself with fewer bookings and clients which would have given me more private time but not the income.

What advice do I give others when they ask about finding their life partner? "Work on your self. What do you like to do? Do you even know? Do what you want to do, what makes you happy. Only in following your heart will your path become clear to you."

What would Michael say about relationship? For one thing, probably more than we have space for in this post script. He might say that he had given up on meeting his mate, that everyone he dated wanted to change him. So he decided to do what he liked; skiing, white water kayaking, scuba-diving, spiritual searching, to mention a few things. If a woman came along who enjoyed those things, great! If not, then he would be happy doing what he liked to do, and he would be true to himself.

If you had asked me if I liked the things he liked to do, I wouldn't say that I did (with the exception of the search). They were, for the most part, foreign to me. However, Michael brought out the adventuresome part of myself that I had stuffed for most of my adult life. Obviously, we connected on the spiritual search, and by being with Michael I discovered that physical movement and activity are also part of the search.

Travels

Remember the movie "Always?" When asked if humans could hear those who weren't in physical form the Angel replied, "Yes. It's a thought and they think it's their thought."

I think that this is the way we receive communication. It's just a thought or a feeling of a thought. We think it is our own, and it is, but it comes from a higher part of ourselves, a part that can see the totality of the situation.

In the fall of 1988, Michael and I decided that we wanted to go on a trip to Peru. We contacted our travel agent at least six months prior to our planned March departure date. Every month following our initial contact, we called to see if she had information for us, or ask, "Why haven't we received any brochures on South America and Peru?" As February rolled around, we were beginning to become concerned, as we had nothing in hand for all of our efforts.

One last call to the agent resulted in our ascertaining that all of the flights were booked and there was no way that we would make it south that spring.

"How can this be? We've been calling you for months! You have had our planned itinerary. What happened?" Needless to say, we were upset. The agent had more than ample time to book tickets for us for the dates we wanted to travel.

Michael began to call airlines and, after several hours, managed to find a couple of seats, albeit inconvenient travel times, that would get us to our destination and back. In the meantime, I began to call for information about Peru. I began with the State Department, where I received the following message: "Bombings, explosions, many unforeseen dangers. Travel advisory is not to go to Peru unless absolutely necessary!"

Things were not flowing. I believe that when you are in harmony with the Universe and on your path, things just flow. This was definitely **not flow.** I mentioned my concerns to Michael.

"Don't you believe that if we are to be all right we will be, and if it is our time to step out, then so be it? What about your white light?"

White light. What did I believe about the white

light? Couldn't we go anyway and have things be okay? These thoughts and more were running through my head, when I picked up an *EarthStar* magazine and saw that there was an article by a man, in fact a neighbor, who conducted tours to Peru. I read the article, found it interesting, and tossed it aside. Sometime later I mentioned the article to Michael.

"Great! Let's call him and see what he can tell us." Michael dialed the number. I listened to one side of the conversation.

"No, I don't speak Spanish. You did! Shining Light . . . hmmmm. You wouldn't? No, I've never been to Glastonbury."

After hanging up the phone, he confirmed what I had suspected. "He said, don't go. Especially if you don't speak Spanish, which he does. On his last trip he was face to face with a machine gun and fortunately, because he spoke Spanish, was able to talk himself out of the situation. He asked if we had been to Glastonbury, England. He even mentioned a place to stay. Did you realize that could be how the white light works? Sometimes it just stops the flow in the direction you are attempting."

I hadn't thought of it, white light, Guidance, whatever you want to call it, in that way before. Now I could see that everything is **Intent.** Our inner voice sometimes directs us in a different manner from what we expect. If we keep not hearing, the *voice* comes through someone else. When we kept insisting on going to Peru, the voice of the spirit had to manifest itself in other, more obvious ways.

That same day an old friend Ann called from Washington and out of the blue said, "Have you ever been to Glastonbury?"

"No, but I have a feeling that we're going soon," I replied.

We had lots of frequent flyer mileage, but we

didn't have the certificates in hand. We wanted to leave for our trip within two weeks. Of course we managed to get the certificates, flights and seats that we wanted, and within two weeks we were in merry old England. Things couldn't haven't gone more smoothly. Another message of the spirit . . . things were flowing smoothly.

Although Michael and I had planned to marry in Maine in the fall, we always said that if we found a magical place we would get married there. Glastonbury was such a place, but it seemed that we hadn't learned our lessons about flow and harmony; so we had to repeat them. Actually, it was more of a lesson in letting go of logic and trusting that we were in the right place at the right time. How could we have doubted it?

It appeared that there were several obstacles in our path to an English wedding. We were both divorced, and the British didn't necessarily believe that American divorces were legal (my interpretation); we had to have a residence there; because we were divorced we could only be married by the Registrar, and because it was Easter he was quite booked up. At first, we thought we would have the Head Druid or someone similar do a ceremony for us, and then we would have it legalized. No one could tell us just who the Head Druid was. It wasn't as though it was a secret; there were several who made claims to the title, but others wouldn't confirm this. At one point I found myself setting up a meeting with an Episcopalian priest, which was the last thing that I wanted. After all the running around, I gave up and decided that it wasn't supposed to happen.

On the way back to our bed and breakfast, in the pouring rain, we stopped by the Chalice Well. I'm not sure why we stopped at this particular time, perhaps because this is the well of healing waters, and, so the myth says, the Holy Grail is buried there. It certainly seemed that at times we were searching for the Grail. Inside the small British cottage there were many wonderful books, herbs, and other "remedies" to soothe the soul. We spent time making our book selections, as usual far more than we would be able to read. One could say that we were adding just more weight to our already heavy bags! As we prepared to leave, we met Willa, the Warden of the Well.

"What are you two ducks doing out in this weather? Is there something I can help you with?"

Now, knowing Willa as I do, I am certain that she knew what we were trying to do long before she verbally asked the question. We explained that we wanted to get married in England and it seemed as if the obstacles were insurmountable. For one, we needed to be in residence there.

"You can use my home as your residence. I'll write it down for you."

Still not convinced this would work, I put the paper she handed me in my bag and we headed out. That night we decided, once again, that this was not flowing, it was more effort than need be, and that we would head to Scotland in the morning. We snuggled into our bed and fell asleep in each other's arms, listening to the sound of the rain. "I wonder if this really was (or is) Camelot? I'll think about it in the morning . . . "

Breakfast at *Tor Down* B and B. As we entered the dining room, we noticed that there was only one other guest eating breakfast, a large, dark haired, quite friendly man.

"Good Morning. And just what brings you to Glastonbury?"

"We're just trying to get married," Michael replied.

I could have fallen off my chair; in fact if I hadn't been already firmly planted on the seat I probably would have. Who was the man who said we were trying to get married? Certainly not Michael because he didn't talk of these things to strangers, at least not in the first two minutes after meeting them.

I don't remember the exact words of what the Stranger said. I do know that I felt he was channeling the message just for us. It sounded familiar, the essence of it was, "If you want something you have to go for it."

Until one is committed, there is hesitancy, the chance to draw back, always ineffectiveness.

Concerning all acts of initiative (and creation), there is one elementary truth, the ignorance of which kills countless ideas and splendid plans: that the moment one definitely commits oneself, then Providence moves too.

All sorts of things occur to help one that never would otherwise have occurred. A whole stream of events issues from the decision, raising in one's favor all manner of unforeseen incidents and meetings and material assistance, which no man could have dreamed would have come his way.

Whatever you can do, or dream you can, Begin it.
Boldness has genius, power and magic in it.
Begin it now.

                                                            Goethe

Did this man really look similar to my image of Goethe? Or am I just filling in the blanks in my mind?

"Going for it." If you really want something you have to first commit. We weren't really committed to this thing of marriage. To each other yes, to the societal concept of marriage, no. If we were, we would have put out the energy to "go for it!"

Before our breakfast friend had finished speaking, we were pushing our chairs back from the table, knowing that we were on our way to the registrar's office to give him our divorce decrees so that they could be mailed to London for approval. Even to this day we question, "Why marry? For society? Government? Children? That day the issue was really commitment, and this man, from wherever he came (he said the Isle of Man), gave us a message about commitment.

When the registrar asked for our address, I pulled out the small, blue paper that Willa had written her address on the previous evening. "Little St. Michael's Chalice Well." A chill ran through me because I knew we were on the path of the spirit once more. I also knew that London would approve of our papers and allow us to be married there, and I knew that even though the weeks were crowded, the Registrar would have a slot when he could perform the legal ceremony.

We jumped into our Metro, a rollerskate of a car, and headed to Scotland. As we left Glastonbury, I reflected on how we seemed to have stepped back in time to the legend of King Arthur. There were so many things that seemed familiar it was uncanny. Was it coincidence that I was here in Avalon with a man named Michael Arthur? What was my role in the myth? None of the characters I remembered seemed to fit (although I thought of Morgan le Fay). Or, perhaps my role was that of a figure unknown to the world today.

I decided to give Michael a sword as a wedding present.

Yes, Glastonbury was, and still is, definitely a magical place for us.

Scotland

As soon as we crossed the border into Scotland I developed a chill that I couldn't get rid of, and I remember commenting on the very different energy of the country.

Try as I might, I was never able to get warm the entire time I was there. I later decided that it was because of all of the individuals tortured and burned there in the past as witches . . . thousands.

It was while in Scotland that Michael and I had the first of what are our more serious emotional upheavals.

"Why are we getting married?" Michael asked. "Who are we getting married for? Are we getting married just for society? Do we need society's stamp of approval for our commitment?"

I asked myself why did I want to be married? Would I feel any more secure? No. Yes. Maybe. Maybe not. What then? I was still a woman from the South, hanging on to some paradigms I didn't want to let go of. I had never ever met anyone like Michael; I had never felt this way before about anyone. Would a piece of paper from some strangers make me feel any different? I would later learn that this was just the beginning of the "looking into myself," being reflected back by my mate.

Upheavals like this hurt. Did I really want to let someone get so close to me that he could affect my emotions in this way? I am certain that a part of me, the vulnerable child, would say, "Probably not," but the part that had brought us together in the first place was saying, "You have to. You have no choice."

Glastonbury

As events came to pass, what we feel is our real wedding and commitment to each other came with just the two of us present. Our "legal" British ceremony was scheduled for March 22, but we decided that we wanted to be married March 20 at the exact time of the equinox. We planned everything very carefully, down to when and where I would buy my flowers and what type of wine goblets we would purchase to drink the water from the Chalice well.

Typical of England, we awoke to a sunny, and yet misty, spring morning. As we looked out across the down, we could imagine what it must have been like in times past. However, within minutes before we were to begin our ceremony, the clouds looked as if they could compete with those that floated Noah's Ark.

In our preparations, we selected the head of the Chalice Well as the location of our commitment to each other. Prepared for rain, we went about settling in, with our flowers, goblets and other assorted items for our ritual. All of a sudden I looked up and Willa, the Warden of the Well, was hastily walking toward us.

"We have a room inside where I think you'll be more comfortable for your ceremony."

I wasn't prepared for another decision. This was changing my "flow," my idea of how the day would go. Michael and I had decided to hold our ritual at the head of the well, and she was suggesting something else. I looked down at the intertwined symbol of two circles on the cover of the well and found myself torn between the reasons I thought I wanted to be married at this particular spot and my feeling that my Higher Self was presenting us another, perhaps more comfortable option, one that would at least be dry.

Willa smiled, obviously knowing my dilemma. "You can always change your mind."

Why do I always feel as if this woman whom I call Willa is looking deep inside of me?

Thoughts raced through my mind, but one stood

out: "She's right. We'll look at the room and if we don't like it we can come back out here."

We followed Willa into a lovely English Tudor home that stood on the Chalice Well grounds. Strange that I hadn't given it much attention prior to that moment. "What an interesting combination, very Zen-like, sparsely but elegantly decorated," I thought, as she led us to a dark, walnut polished staircase that wound up and up. When we approached the top landing, my eyes became riveted to the door in front of me as I gazed upon a painting of a beautiful sword. I blinked several times and moved closer to make sure that my contact lenses weren't failing me. Was I really reading "Saint Michael" written under the sword? Tears of excitement rolled down my cheeks as I realized that this was the sword that I had been looking for ever since we decided to get married in England. I had searched in every antique store, flea market and military store I could find as we traveled through Wales, Scotland and Ireland, not to mention the rest of England. All to no avail. I couldn't find it because it wasn't a sword that I was supposed to purchase, but it was a sword from the future.

Behind this door was a beautiful room with yellow stained glass windows and a long oriental carpet running down the center, covering the hardwood floor. Willa had placed a circle of spring flowers in the center of the carpet. When we entered she bent down and lit a candle which was standing in the middle of the flowers. Throughout the rest of the room were candles and incense, and when we looked to our right we saw, through a sheer veil, a wooden rail which separated a table set for the Last Supper, another part of the Glastonbury legend. This part looked so real it could have been the model for the painting of The Last Supper.

As Willa left and closed the door behind her,

161

Michael took my hand and we took our place on the carpet, wondering if we had stepped back in time. It really didn't matter, for on this day, in this magical place, we made our commitment to each other.

I did manage to manifest a sword in the flesh, or metal as one might say. We met an arms and armor dealer who struck up a friendship with my new husband. They had much in common, including the flying of airplanes. Ron invited us to visit him if we should be in Devon.

It seemed that within the blinking of an eye we did find ourselves in Devon, in Ron's home. When we entered his sitting room, our eyes immediately fell on the most magnificent sword we had seen, other than in the Tower of London. It was his prize, but he was willing to part with it, reluctantly, on the condition that if we ever wanted to sell it, we would sell it back to him. It now hangs over our fireplace as a reminder of our time in Camelot and that, for us, there is still magic in the world.

Paris

There are times when we have to let go of something that we think we want (Peru), and there are times we have to go for something that we think is going to be hard (getting married in a foreign country). What was the difference for us? The doors to Peru continually shut. Getting there didn't flow, no matter how hard we tried to force it. At the other extreme, we shut the doors to getting married without trying. We let the rules and regulations get in our way. Once we decided to pursue a British marriage, things flowed easily. We had to make up our mind about what we wanted. We had to commit.

From England we flew to Paris for a wonderful week of experiencing the senses. The *joie de vivre* is truly a way of living with the French; food, wine, flowers, music—all of the senses are constantly stimulated!

At 5:00 Good Friday, Michael and I unexpectedly found ourselves at Notre Dame. As we watched the hundreds of people go into the cathedral, we realized that this was a special mass; so we stepped inside to observe. Notre Dame was packed with 9,000 individuals. Never have I felt such energy! This was one of those experiences that can only be lived; words could not do it justice. It reminded me that life is energy and spirit, and spirit is everywhere, including in traditional religion. We joined in the spirit and thanked our spirits while lighting candles.

Our time in Paris was all too short. I love Paris . . .

The night before we were to fly home, I had one of my precognitive dreams. I had fallen asleep early in the evening while Michael was still reading, and the sense of the dream was very real. We were in de Gaulle airport getting ready to go to our gate, when there was a loud explosion; clearly a bomb had gone off! I awoke with a start, which caused Michael to jump and ask me what was going on. My first thought centered on what do I do? This dream followed the pattern of my dreams that have been precognitive. I thought about creating one's reality and tried to decide which came first, the bomb, or my dream that a bomb was going to go off. I thought that if I told Michael, he would then add his energy to my dream or thoughts and increase the probability of its taking place. I decided to do nothing but surround the entire situation with white light, and ask for help. I had to believe that we were, and would be, exactly where we were supposed to be at any given time.

The next morning I began to put our documents in order; plane tickets, passports . . .

"Michael, do you have your passport?"

"No, you still have it."

Maybe we wouldn't be leaving after all if I had lost or allowed his passport to be stolen. No, there it was, hidden in a pocket. It appeared that we were on our way to de Gaulle after all.

Because this was a time of heightened security, given the world situation, there were many announcements about leaving baggage unattended. I kept looking to see if Salman Rusdhie was lurking in the wings.

We had an uneventful departure.

Upon arriving in London, we learned that a fake bomb had been left on one of the British Airways planes following a training class with the search dogs. Was this what I had sensed? Had I changed the original message of the dream? Was the dream telling me something entirely different? I don't know. I am happy to be sitting here right now recounting this story.

Do we have the power to change things we dream or think are going to happen? I have to think we do, or else our belief that we create our reality falls apart. There are many times when our beliefs or paradigms get tested, and there are times when it is possible that what we did acted as an agent of change. Perhaps, as Michael Talbot wrote in the *Holographic Universe,* there are many parallel realities and we jump from one to another when we change what appears to be a certain outcome.

Home

After I moved in with Michael, he began to feel that it was time to leave the beach and look for more land. I, on the other hand, loved the beach, the roughness of the Maine coastline, being able to let the dogs run freely. And I loved, at long last, being in a home. This was a real home, not a piece of rental property. I could plant flowers and make gardens and put my energy into the earth here, knowing that next year the flowers would come up, not the rent.

This is not to say that Michael didn't love the beach; if ever there was man who loved the ocean, nature and the beach it's Michael. What he did not like were the crowds that descended upon us by May. At first I tried to ignore the masses of people and I did a fairly decent job of doing so.

For a year and a half Michael looked at the real estate ads in the Sunday paper looking for land. We contacted several agents who, for one reason or another, either didn't take us seriously or thought that we could afford more than our budget. Every time we had the opportunity to conduct psychic readings, (sessions which would usually come at the end of my intuitive medical readings), Michael would ask, "Where is our land?"

The reply, usually, "Keep looking."

One day Michael asked if he would get our land through an agent.

"No."

"Then through the newspaper?"

"No."

"Then what am I supposed to do? Why am I wasting my time with newspapers and agents?"

"Keep looking."

I received bits and pieces of psychic pictures, nothing I could identify as a specific location. We were told that initially there would not be as much land as we would like, but that there would be more available from a farmer.

One day, very frustrated, Michael looked at me with his *Why are you creating this?* look and said, "Why are we not finding our land?" Unfortunately, we both knew why. I was not ready to give up the beach, and I didn't have the desire to move that he did. Amazing how quickly things can change. In less than two days I was ready to move. I stood in our living room and watched what seemed to be hundreds of beachgoers walk by and stare. I felt that I had no privacy. Within my spirit I felt a tremendous release of our beach cottage and I was ready to move on.

In order to prove to ourselves that we were ready to truly let go of the cottage, Michael and I had a *For Sale* sign made.

During one of the next sessions, Michael asked, "Where is our property?"

"Buxton" came the reply. I had previously seen a river with foam on it, which I interpreted to be the Saco River in Maine. To me the foam indicated that the river met the ocean. I had also seen what seemed to be a shack on the land.

"You can't live in it."

"We haven't looked in Buxton."

We were soon on our way to the Township of Buxton . . . looking for land. We had been up and down the Saco River on the opposite side and had not been successful. Now we were off again.

As we wound our way down the beautiful country road that followed the deep bends in the Saco river, we passed through several quaint New England villages. I remember that the village of Bar Mills seemed to take me back in time. However, our luck with finding property seemed to be nonexistent this day.

On our way home we happened to see a *For Sale by Builder* sign on a little cedar house in the woods. We weren't looking for a home, as we planned to design and build our own, not to mention the fact we didn't feel we could afford a house. Still, out of curiosity, we drove up. I got out of the car, walked around the front of the house and looked down into this beautiful virgin cove. The feeling that came over me was indescribable. I knew that I wanted this place; it was unlike any place I had ever seen. It was as though the energy of the land and water reached out and grabbed me. When we walked inside I stopped and stared, for there was a huge stone fireplace in what would eventually be a very bright and sunny room. At least ten years previously, I had started seeing in my mind's eye a home that was in the woods with hardwood floors and a huge stone fireplace. The home was very bright and sunny, and although I called it a log cabin, I couldn't put the pieces together of how it could be so bright and still be a cabin. Now I knew. It wasn't a cabin, it was a little cedar house with a cathedral ceiling.

Our first impression was that the living room was too small. My piano would never fit in there. In fact, the house itself was small. But the location!

After we returned to the beach I found that I couldn't get the home in the woods out of my mind. I pushed Michael to call the builder and see what he was asking for it.

The next day, at sunset, we returned to the house in the woods for a closer look and, though usually it was locked, someone had left the front door open. We walked in to see a crimson sunset. The entire inside of the house was colored with beautiful shades of pink and rose from the setting sun, which was descending directly over the lake. This view was unbelievable. By now we were hooked, and I began to be afraid that someone would come by and buy it on the spot.

"If it's ours it will be there," Michael kept telling me. I knew he was right; there were so many things that said this was the place I had been creating for years, that I had to trust we would have it. If not, something better would come along.

We looked at other land along the Saco, none of which lived up to the location of the house in the woods. We negotiated, agreed to take out a wall, stood back, signed a contract, and then became terribly, terribly anxious.

I worried that I was becoming a wife who wanted a house at all costs, even at the cost of her husband taking a job he didn't want in order to have the house.

Michael worried that we would be house-poor. All of our resources would go into the house, and we would have little or nothing liquid. (As it turned out, he was right.) We looked at our finances again and again. At the same time, Michael was realizing that this was, with a couple of minor exceptions, the house he had been mentally creating, while listening to me lead guided imagery meditations in my workshops.

After a week of virtually no sleep and lots of anxious moments, I asked, "What will we do if we don't buy this house?" to which Michael replied,

"We will keep looking for land."

This was an excellent opportunity for us to experience another area of goal setting and creating. What happens when you get what you ask for? We didn't ask that our land or home be free. We just asked that we find it within our price range. It was scary. We found what we were creating, but there was a point where we had to make a decision on whether or not to go through with *the purchase.* We asked ourselves another question, "What is the worst thing that can happen?"

"We'll lose everything."

"So?"

"We'll just start over. We created it once; we can certainly do it again."

I believe that. The more you create something, the stronger you become in creating, like baking a cake. Practice makes perfect.

Price includes a lot more than the cost of the house, and we are presently working to be debt-free. (In the appendix you will find a book entitled: *Your Money or Your Life* which I highly recommend. This book forms the basis for many of our attitudes and beliefs about money and freedom.)

We still love the house and the location, and although there are some things which we would do differently, we would do it again.

The Blessing of the Land (The Sweat Lodge)

Our land, which is very sacred to us, is land that is strongly Native American. This can be said of most of Maine, but where we live at the moment is very undeveloped, and the spirit of the past residents is very evident.

During a workshop I conducted, I met a man who had lived with the Lakota Indians.

When I spoke of my feelings for the "Warrior" that was ever present on our land, he suggested that we conduct a special ceremony to contact him and create a sacred space. This sounded very exciting to me and I readily agreed.

Six months later, Michael and I found ourselves with eight wonderful individuals who had come together to help build our sweat lodge. I thought it interesting that I awoke with a terrible sore throat, which I attributed to the pollen count that day. Why didn't I ask myself what was the emotional source of the sore throat?

The first thing we did was head to the local dispatch to obtain a fire permit. This time they denied us the permit because the wind was blowing strongly, but they said to return at 6pm and see what the weather conditions were then. (We live in the middle of a very thick, 200-acre pine and hardwood forest.) Our *sweat leader* said that we would construct the lodge anyway and have it ready; we could always hold a pipe ceremony.

At 6:00 p.m. we finished the lodge, and by now the wind was blowing harder than ever. We returned to the dispatch to see if we could obtain the permit, while back at the sweat lodge prayers were said asking for guidance and help. No one could have been more surprised than Michael and I when we were handed the fire permit for the next six hours.

We returned to the site, and the workers began to lay an incredible fire of pine logs and kindling. The pile must have been five feet tall. Needless to say, I began to get nervous. My throat, which had been very sore, was still very sore. I decided that the sweat would do a lot of good for my sore throat and for Michael's back, which he had twisted.

When the fire was lit, the flames roared up and sparks began to fly everywhere, especially into a pile of dry sticks and rubbish which was very close by. "What have I done?" I asked myself. "This is a very dangerous situation. Is a sweat lodge worth burning down the forest?"

As the flames continued to soar upward, I knew I had to bring water to the pile of brush and wet it down. I also knew that if we needed our garden hose, it would not reach, and even if it did, there would not be enough water in our well lines to be of significant use.

I began to lug heavy buckets of water out to the lodge and to wet down everything in sight. I found myself becoming very annoyed and upset.

"Don't worry; the leader is a good fire person," a friend said as she tried to comfort me. I knew I was not being calm, but for some reason it didn't matter. I began to think of all the creatures that the forest was home to, and we were the caretakers of the forest. As the fire tender piled more logs onto what I thought was already a tenuous situation, I found myself saying that I wanted the fire to burn down a bit. The tender continued to put logs on the fire, and our "leader" continued to work on the lodge.

After many buckets of water, and after pulling the

brush away from the flames, I began to relax. The fire began to die down, as did the winds, and when the sparks came out they went toward our green leach bed for the septic system.

"The fire spirits have tested you to see if you have faith in them."

My first thoughts were, "I certainly failed that test; I had no faith in them not to burn down the forest."

I kicked myself for twenty-four hours about my lack of faith in the fire spirits, when finally my inner voice woke me up, "Of course you don't have faith in the fire spirits; you don't believe in them; they are not part of your paradigm. You believe in yourself, your responsibility and your power, not some external power of fire spirits! It was your inner voice hearing the voice of the forest. This is not to say that the fire spirits are not a valid part of the sweat leader's belief system."

When I came to this realization my sore throat went away.

I began to see the light. Just because I was having a sweat did not mean I had to live all of the beliefs of Native Americans. There are many things in their belief system that I do believe, but there are also just as many things I do not. Perhaps my Cherokee heritage and past life remembrances of being a Native American got in the way of this life and my common sense. Could I have lived with the concept of fire spirits wanting the forest burned down if that had happened? Could I have lived with myself?

Tests, yes. But not by the fire spirits. Why was I giving away my power, and the responsibility of our land, home to so many wonderful creatures, to someone else and their belief system? Not only that, why was I giving my power to someone who didn't have the Native American blood that I did? Why didn't I just say, "The fire is too big. I want it smaller and made with hard wood?" I bet that my sore throat would have instantly vanished and Michael's back felt better if he had "backed up" his true feelings.

The sweat ceremony itself was marvelous; it was such a cleansing ritual, one that I will look forward to again and again. Next time I will control the fire, not let it control me. I now know that we can create intense heat in a lodge with no physical heat source at all.

It's all intent.

I thought that I had worked through my tendency to give my power away, but I can see that I haven't . . . I still have work to do.

Annis Iniby says that there are only three facts of life that we need to live by:

> **Show up.**
> **Be aware (listen).**
> **Tell the truth and don't be attached to the outcome.**

I had shown up. Being there was not the problem.

I was listening, but I was ignoring what I was hearing from my inner voice.

I didn't tell the leaders the truth of what I was feeling and sensing, and I was too attached to the outcome. "Our sweat leader will think that I'm not spiritual if I show that I don't trust the fire spirits by asking that the fire be smaller."

At some point we learn that it doesn't matter what someone else thinks. What matters is what we think ourselves.

Life is either one dangerous adventure or nothing at all.

Helen Keller

Most of us tend to live our lives as safely as possible, hopeful that we won't do anything that will bring harm to our bodies. Have you ever considered how limiting this concept can be? What if you are one of those individuals who is afraid to fly in an airplane because it might crash? Think of all the places in the world that you are excluding from your life experiences because you can't get there.

I have noticed that there are many individuals who let their beliefs about age do the limiting for them. Saying, "I'm too old to do that," can be a wonderful way of not living. (I recently met a 12-year-old who thought he was too old to water ski.) I am blessed with a wonderful sixty-four-year-old mother-in-law who water skiis on one ski, downhill skiis, rides horseback, and does anything else she darn well pleases. She is a good role model for me. There is a saying in the family that I married into, "Winter doesn't do it, yet!" As I check off the things I am learning to do now, in my early forties, I have come to love the word "yet," because it is full of anticipation and expectancy. What, after all, is life? Is it working all day from nine to five, racing to the grocery store for fast food for dinner, and then collapsing in front of the television because you are too tired to do anything else? Does your work make you happy? Do you refuse to do things just because you haven't done them before? You are spending a great many hours of your lifetime doing something that, hopefully, you enjoy.

Where do you start? Change comes from inside; we have to change our way of thinking. I believe that we first begin to pay attention to all of the voices (or family) that live within us. There is always one voice (our creative child) that sees new opportunities for growth, for fun, for expansion of awareness. This voice may be subtle if you have not listened to it for a while. Once this voice speaks, there is another, the critic, the parent, the controller, that will tell you just why you can't, or shouldn't, do whatever it is that you desire to do. Pay attention to the two voices; just listen. Where did they come from? What are you afraid of? What is the worst thing that could happen if you follow that voice of the creative child?

As you begin to learn new things, you will find a freedom you may not have felt since you were a child.

Sailing

When Michael and I first began to date, he decided that he wanted us to rent a sailboat (bareboat) and sail the Virgin Islands. I was excited at the same time that I was terrified. I had been sailing many times, but never **really** sailing where I was crew. I knew how to duck my head when the skipper yelled, "Coming about," and I knew how to release the sheets. I reflected back to numerous "Captains" I had known who were really bastards, not at all nice to those who were on the boat. I wondered what Michael would be like as "Captain" and if this relationship would survive ten days, alone, together, on the sea.

We had not been sailing many days when we encountered our first storm and Michael had to bring down the mainsheet. For him to be able to do this, I had to take the helm and head the boat into the wind. I had done this many times before and didn't think much of it, until I actually took hold of the wheel and found that the ocean was quite rough and the winds strong. I decided that I didn't like it.

"Michael, I don't want to do this anymore."

The response came back quickly: "Winter, you've got to. There's no one else on the boat!"

End of **Lesson One** in sailing: The amount of work to be done at any one time is not directly proportional to the number of crew members.

Lesson Two: Bringing a sailboat into a slip in a marina next to a very expensive yacht came shortly on the heels of lesson one.

It seemed easy enough. Michael would slowly pull the boat into the slip and I would jump over the safety line to the dock and tie it up. Me, who grew up in the mountains of North Carolina as the original mountain goat, and me, the adult of the young girl who used to walk on the inside safety rail of the swimming pool and occasionally fall out of the pool. I poised on the bow ready to take my leap, my deck shoes firmly in place on the bow of the Beneteau.

"You must move quickly because I don't want to hit this other boat," Michael reminded me.

We pulled in and I stepped across the wire. I froze. I couldn't move my right foot across the wire to the dock. What was wrong? Michael gave me a look that said, "I can't believe you're doing that," as we moved closer and closer to a quick encounter with both the dock and the expensive yacht. No matter how hard I tried, I found that I was unable to place both feet on the dock. I was able, however, to place both feet back on the boat.

Fortunately, there was an angel on the dock in the form of a man who had been watching the whole scene, who came to our rescue, grabbed the line and tied up the boat.

I had thought that this trip would be very relaxed; we would sail and discuss spiritual matters. At last we would be able to talk about Carlos Castaneda and the meaning of life. Wrong; the trip was non-stop. Having only two individuals to man a thirty-six foot sailboat does not allow for a great amount of leisure time if there is wind. By the half-way mark of the first day, I gave up the idea of spiritual talk and began to recognize a confidence in myself that I had not seen in a long time. I was doing things I had not done before, things that in some ways could be seen as dangerous, and I was loving every moment of it. Our routine changed; we went to bed shortly after dark and got up with the sun. Our lives were changing.

Not until we were back in Logan Airport in Boston did I realize what a tune-up I had undergone with my intuition. I instantly knew things, such as where to find our friend who was to pick us up.

Our sailing adventure enabled me to see important elements to developing one's intuition; stay in the *now* (this is something that is easier to do when you are with nature and the elements.) Now means survival, because in many instances you are in the moment in what you are doing and you are anticipating the future in terms of weather, moorings, etc. Being on the water brings me in touch with all of this. I have also come to realize that it is impossible to be anything but in the now when you are with a dolphin. To be with them you must be one hundred and one percent present.

These days, it is not unusual for me to tend our boat while Michael is scuba diving. I value this time when I am alone, watching, thinking, pondering the ocean and its mysteries.

Just Do it

I am constantly learning that there are things we have to "just do" in order to get past our blocks and fears. We can talk about doing something all we want, but talk, as the saying goes, is cheap. There comes a time when we have to do!

This "just doing" is true in manifesting and creating those things that we desire. Energy has to be put forth in order for things to show up in the material world. For example, what is it that you would like to create in your life? A new job? A relationship? A trip? These things are not created in isolation; each is in some way related to the other. I think it is important to remember that we have a brain, hands, feet, emotions—many elements that are essential for creating what we desire. The act of creating uses all of our

176

abilities.

I have come a long way since our first sailing trip. I can put on my scuba gear and go over the side of a boat in open ocean and meet up with Michael who is already on the bottom. I can also go over the side of a boat in a rough open ocean without my scuba gear. And, I have confidence in my handling of a sailboat in a storm. I still don't like it, but I can do it.

Sometimes you think that you are on the wrong road when you are actually on the right road. There are no signs along the way until you are almost to the end, but by now you have spoiled the trip by all of the worrying that you did thinking that you are on the wrong road!

Joe Rhames
Friend and Philosopher

There are many times when we miss the scenery because we are afraid we are on the wrong road. In fact, we may miss the entire trip because we are afraid to follow our gut feelings and follow what may seem like an unknown way.

What difference does it make which road we are on? Will Rogers once said, *"Even if you are on the right track, you'll get run over if you just sit there."* Is there ever a wrong road, or even a wrong turn for that matter? I think not. It is my belief that as long as we are aware that we are on a road at all, the implication is that we are moving. Much time and energy are spent while we consider if we are on the right path. I think that we are always on the right track. It is how we perceive the scenery and the individuals that we meet along the path that makes the difference.

You'll never see yourself, except through a reflection.

Michael Robinson

There is one more element to this story that needs to be included; the stormy side of relationships. Until now I have written about the wonderful, magical world of love and relationship. The laws of nature say that there must be another side in order to balance, a side which is sometimes called the shadow. I refer to the shadow as the storm, because storms have clouds and clouds, of course, cast shadows. Storms are necessary for the rain which nurtures the land and all living things.

Michael and I each have a stormy side which we sometimes show to each other. This is a part of what and who we are. It is important to write about, because I am finding that many individuals who think they have found their perfect love are appalled when they find themselves in the middle of a storm. Somewhere in their fantasy world, which probably came from the movies, they have decided that if people are in love, deeply in love, then they don't argue . . . they don't disagree.

Storms and arguments are a side of relationships that can be effective for growth, if we take time to look honestly at what is happening. This means that we can't get hooked into being the victim or trying to control the other. *Our significant other* is our reflection, a way to journey inward; and my belief says that it is unrealistic to think that once you are in a meaningful relationship there won't be differences and disagreements. We are still in two different bodies; we have different life experiences prior to coming together and different thoughts about our lives, separately and together.

The scariest thing about arguments is the feeling of separateness, of being alone, perhaps, of feeling not loved. All of our issues of abandonment and vulnerability come rising to the surface and we create the thought, "What would life be without this person?"

If we have made a decision to learn in a relationship, we have made a commitment to see ourselves as clearly as we can. We can always leave someone else, but we can't leave ourselves. As we commit to our inner growth, and then to our significant other, we commit to all relationships, with the earth, with nature, with the universe. Remember, "When one definitely commits oneself, then Providence moves too."

A New Paradigm

This last section is about paradigms, men and magic. In writing a book, it is important to know when to stop and when to keep going. I feel it is time to stop, but as I do I want to include some new "food for thought."

I think the "guidelines" are wrong about how men and women feel, communicate and intuit information. All of us are so caught in the old paradigms of typecasting, we fail to see that we are in the era of the *new man* who is trying very hard to allow his sensitive, caring and intuitive side to emerge. He is a man who is trying to find his way in life, not to be tied to a nine-to-five job that is taking his life away. He is a man who realizes the role men have played in society and in relationships for hundreds of years. He knows, and he seeks a way to change things.

I can almost hear you now, asking me where these men are because you haven't met them.

One premise of this book is that everything is a reflection of ourselves. What occurs inside us is reflected in our surroundings and environment. If we can't see the sensitivity in the opposite sex, perhaps we can't see it inside ourselves. All of us have the yin and the yang, the active and the passive energies. Are you sensitive enough to allow yourself to be vulnerable and still be strong? To not "need" a man (or a woman) for security? Can you be comfortable in not trying to control someone, but in allowing them to be themselves, whatever that self may be? Can you be comfortable in the knowledge that this man is the male side of yourself (or woman is the female side of yourself), reflecting your active or passive energy?

You see, it is my opinion that men are greatly misunderstood when it comes to intuition. They may be the more intuitive and creative of the species, but they are just not as adept as bringing these thoughts and feelings forward. In our society men were taught at a young age that it wasn't manly to show sensitive emotions; anger, perhaps, but not sadness or other "soft" feelings. If we remember men were once hunters in the wild and had to be able to sense their prey, we realize that deep within them this sense is still there.

Because we expect men to be logical and analytical from the time they are small, all of their thoughts of magic, spirit, the universe, and nature are either stuffed or talked about in technical terms. As children, they had dreams and imaginations, too. Their bikes could fly, their fingers shoot bullets, and their closets held monsters, just like ours. As they grew up, they frequently carried their imagination and creativity into their working world, sometimes to build buildings, homes and shopping centers. Other times their imagination motivated them to take things apart, to see how things work.

As girls, our imaginations were tied up with everything; dolls and birds, snakes and Indians, fairies and magic homes among the trees, invisible playmates and thoughts of a prince who would one day ride up on his white horse, just like the one in Cinderella.

So, what happened to our prince on the white horse, or our princess in the ivory tower? They were human, just like us; we just couldn't see it because it wasn't part of the fairy tale.

Why can't we see each other as we really are? Why do we have to blame someone else for our difficulties? Because we have allowed the magic we once knew to be diminished by the limiting beliefs of others and by our own fears. We have allowed ourselves to forget that we are magical humans, childlike and imaginative, and that we are all doing the best we can. Because we have forgotten this, we get mad at those around us, because we sense that they have also forgotten the magic, and it makes us sad. We need someone to remember with us.

I remember magic, and I want you to remember, while there is still time to use it.

Suggested Reading

Castaneda, Carlos. *The Power of Silence.* New York, N.Y: Simon & Schuster, 1987.

Crichton, Michael. *Travels.* New York, N.Y: Alfred A. Knopf, 1988.

Dominguez, Joe and Vicki Robin. *Your Money or Your Life.* New York, N.Y.: Viking Penguin. 1992,

Figgie, Harry E., Jr. *Bankruptcy, 1995.* Boston, MA: Little, Brown & Company, 1992.

Goldstein, Joseph. *Insight Meditation.* Boston and London: Shambala, 1993.

Kabat-Zinn, John. *Wherever You Go, There You Are.* New York: Hyperion, 1994.

Redfield, James. *Celestine Prophecy.* New York: Time-Warner, 1993.

Robbins, John. *Diet for a New America.* Walpole, NH: Stillpoint, 1987.

Russell, Peter. *The White Hole in Time.* San Francisco, CA: Harper, 1992.

Talbot, Michael. *The Holographic Universe.* New York, NY: Harper Collins, 1991.

McCammon, Robert R. *Boy's Life.* New York, NY: Pocket Books. 1991

Murphy, Michael. *The Future of the Body.* Los Angeles, CA: Jeremy P. Tarcher, Inc. 1992.

Roddick, Anita. *Body and Soul.* New York, NY:
    Crown Publishers, Inc. 1991.

Steinem, Gloria. *Revolution from Within.* Boston, MA:
    Little, Brown & Company, 1992.

Zukav, Gary. *The Seat of the Soul.* New York, NY:
    Simon & Schuster. 1989.

Newsletters and Other Publications

Brain/Mind Bulletin
Box 42211
Los Angeles, CA 90042

Common Boundary
Box 445
Mount Morris, IL 61054

Environmental Nutrition
2112 Broadway
New York, NY 10023

Institute of Noetic Sciences
475 Gate Road, Suite 300,
Sausalito, CA 94965

Nutrition Action Newsletter
CSPI
Suite 300
1875 Connecticut Ave. N.W.
Washington, D.C. 20009-5728

TRANET
Box 567
Rangeley, ME 04970

Organizations Close to My Heart

Dolphin Research Center

P.O. Box 2875
Marathon Shores, FL 33052

The Dolphin Research Center is a not-for-profit research and education organization which manages the only private, non-commercial dolphin facility in North America.

Wild Dolphin Project

21 Hepburn Avenue, Suite 20
Jupiter, FL 33458

The Wild Dolphin Project is a scientific organization which conducts long-term research on dolphin communication and interspecies interaction.

Tor Down Publishing

Thank you for purchasing *Intuitions.* For your convenience we are including this order form for *Intuitions*, the cassette tape by Winter, *Discovering Intuition*, and her newest book, *Remembering.*

~ ORDER FORM ~

Name (Please Print) _____

Mailing Address _____

_____

Please send to the above address _____ copies of

_____ *Intuitions, Seeing with the Heart* priced at $10.95 plus $3.00 (for first title--$1.00 for each additional title)

_____ *Discovering Intuition* cassette priced at $12.95.

_____ *Remembering* priced at $13.95 plus $3.00 (for first title--$1.00 for each additional title)

Send check or money order to:

Tor Down Publishing
430 Simpson Road
Saco, ME 04072

For questions or information call: (207) 929-6960